STEVE OVETT

Portrait of an Athlete

SIMON TURNBULL

A STAR BOOK

published by
the Paperback Division of
W. H. ALLEN & Co. Ltd

A Star Book
Published in 1983
by the Paperback Division of
W. H. Allen & Co. Ltd
A Howard and Wyndham Company
44 Hill Street, London W1X 8LB

First published in Great Britain by W. H. Allen & Co. Ltd, 1982

Printed in Great Britain by
Hunt Barnard Printing, Ltd., Aylesbury, Bucks.

ISBN 0 352 31277 7

To Lesley and Hayley

STEVE OVETT

'Behind the facade of the arrogant extrovert who has the nerve to wave to the crowd whilst setting world records, is another man who shares the same characteristics and anxieties as other less celebrated mortals; a man who is shy and nervy and quite often lazy. What sets Steve Ovett apart from the mass is not only his incredible running talent but also his often unpublicised charity work and, moreover, the fact that he was the first sportsman to turn his back on the public ego-trip which accompanies contemporary superstardom.'

Freelance sports journalist Simon Turnbull, who lives in Newcastle, is North East football correspondent for *The Mail on Sunday*. He writes about athletics for the *Northern Echo* and is a regular contributor to several well-known sporting magazines. *Steve Ovett* is an inspired portrait of one of the world's most intriguing sporting figures.

Contents

Acknowledgements

I would like to thank Stewart Bonney for his invaluable help, research and support in the writing of this book.

I would also like to thank the following: Jacqui Eynon, Dave Simpson, Carol Clewlow, Doug Hall, Michael Scott, Karen Graham, Karen Ripley, Mark Blacklock, Norma Bonney, Mike Bailey, Press Association, *Athletics Weekly, Athletics Monthly, Running Magazine, Track and Field News,* Times Newspapers Ltd., Reg Hook, George Herringshaw, Mike Street, Associated Newspapers Ltd., Stanley Paul Ltd., Sidgwick and Jackson Ltd., BBC TV, ITV, *Sunday Telegraph Magazine, The Observer, Radio Times,* BBC Radio Sport, *Sunday People, Daily Mail,* Associated Press Ltd., Keith Brown, Geoff Smith, Peter Lorenzo, Mel Watman, Barry Trowbridge, Geoff Harrold, Pat Butcher, Dave Cocksedge, Barry Tilbury, Tony Tilbury, Cliff Temple, John Burles, Tony Duffy/Allsports, the late E.D. Lacy, Mrs K. Lacy, the late James Coote, Jon Hendershott, Mike Powell, Peter Francis, John Smith, Lindsay Dunn.

Author's Note

I had hoped Steve Ovett would cooperate in writing this biography but unfortunately he did not feel able to do so. I have therefore had to draw on various interviews he has given over the years for the quotations which are here attributed to him.

Introduction

A Real Wilson of the Wizard

'I hate this attitude the media have that just because someone is good at sport means that their opinion on any topic is of fantastic importance', commented Steve Ovett in an interview with *'ogging* magazine. 'I'm amazed at how many of them get taken in by it. They lose sight of where they're at; get bloated with self-importance. If you get into that situation, you risk spending all your time going around being a famous person. You can get screwed by your own success.'

Such an attitude to public recognition has helped to make Steve Ovett a truly unique figure in world sporting history. It created an air of mystique around one of the greatest ever foot runners, but also earned him the scorn of the British Press. He has been described by various commentators as aloof, brash, arrogant, immature and aggressive and was, until very recently, depicted as a withdrawn, sullen and conceited man who lived an almost hermit-like existence in the backwaters of Brighton.

Many of Ovett's published comments over the years tended to suggest he was never particularly eager to alter that public image. In the same *Jogging* interview, for example, he remarked, 'Sometimes it's good to get away from everyone and everything. Toss a sleeping bag into the Range Rover and drive off somewhere. Those quiet moments when you are alone can be very important to you.' The perpetuation of this Garbo-like image kept the pressures of the Press at arm's length and left Ovett to develop his running talent at his own pace and in his own unburdened manner.

Frank Keating of the *Guardian* once compared Ovett with the spartan athletic heroes from the comic books, 'He has always been a loner — a real Wilson of the Wizard who lopes off into the sunset without waiting to explain himself: not an Alf Tupper, the Tough of the Track, who would have to go to the press conference in the hope of cadging a lift home.'

Yet behind the facade of the arrogant extrovert, who had the nerve to wave to the crowd while setting a new record, has always been another character — the real Steve Ovett. A man who shared the same characteristics and anxieties of other less celebrated mortals. A man who was as shy, nervy and lazy in his private life as he was confident, ruthless and dynamic in the public eye.

What sets Steve Ovett apart from the mass of other sporting stars is not merely his incredible running talent but also his unpublicised charity work and, moreover, the fact that he was the first sportsman to completely turn his back on the public ego trip which accompanies contemporary superstardom. Ovett has consequently been portrayed as a rebel — a 'James Dean of the athletics world' as one journalist put it. But Steve Ovett is in fact a more mellow character: one of the rare breed who can put fame into a balanced perspective.

'I sometimes think about all those people who are ill or crippled and would give anything to walk, let alone run,' he once said. 'Then I realise just how lucky I am. When the training becomes a struggle I often think of that, and it can humble you.' And he recently commented, 'I run because I enjoy it. If you don't enjoy it you're finished, because you can't take the training. But athletics is just a sport. My home and my marriage are far more important.'

This mellow outlook, which Ovett largely hid behind his stern public mask until 1982, prompted *Athletics Weekly*'s editor Mel Watman to describe him as 'a refreshingly free spirit, a young man who doesn't take himself and his sport too seriously, who values his independence and privacy and who runs because he loves to run. In many ways he is the ultimate fun runner.'

There are many descriptions of Steve Ovett. His professed desire to keep a low profile has been counter-productive, prompting innumerable features and articles aimed at dispelling or perpetuating the 'Ovett myth'.

'I am sure he rather enjoys being the anti-hero,' wrote Ovett's former British international team mate Alan Pascoe in his autobiography (*Pascoe*, Stanley Paul, 1979). 'But because he protects the private side of his life so defiantly few realise he is, in fact, very human, talented, emotional and witty. He is a young man of great complexity and, I suspect, insecurity; lately when he has spoken in public while receiving awards he has become quite overcome by the occasion. Yet this is the same man who is so confident on the track — often to the point of arrogance, which makes him appear cold and remote.'

It is precisely this contradictory nature of Steve Ovett's character which intrigues so many observers. Only by detaching himself from the ebullient track showman who courts world attention, can Ovett come to terms with having a public and private life when he is away from the track. Dave Cocksedge has been one of the few journalists with whom Ovett has retained contact over the years — they were very close friends between 1973 and 1979 — and he says of Steve, 'He hides many of his true feelings behind a jesting, bantering manner and a sharp wit.'

There is, of course, another aspect of Steven Michael James Ovett which stimulates great interest. He has developed into one of the two greatest middle distance runners ever to set foot on a running track. His curious surname is derived from the Swedish word for 'owl', a lone hunting bird which tracks its prey before sweeping down on it with a quick burst of speed — the authentic Ovett hallmark!

'His running action exudes the power of his six foot, eleven stone frame, but he has an economic, almost leisurely long stride that disguises a hair-trigger force producing a devastating change of pace that is electrifying to watch,' wrote Ron Pickering in a *Radio Times* article.

'When he catapults past tired runners with vivid acceleration, it is the delayed timing of their response which opens up the gap that is invariably impossible to close. It is the anticipation of it that first makes the crowd hush and then erupt into a cathartic roar. Once the opposition is floundering in his wake, Steve then relaxes to the tape, often with a nonchalant or even arrogant wave to the crowd.'

It is this breath-taking spectacle, akin to Borg on a tennis court, Pele on a football pitch, Ali in the boxing ring, which elevates sport from a desperate battle to come out on top into a distinctive, physical art form. The characters of all these magnificent sportsmen are as intriguing as their actions, for it is undoubtedly their mental capacity which helps to set them apart from 'the rest'.

What is compelling about Steve Ovett is not merely his silver medal in the 1974 European Championships 800m at the age of eighteen, his European Cup 1500m victory the following year, his fifth placing in the Olympic two lap final in 1976, his 1977 World Cup 1500m triumph, his European Championships 1500m gold medal, his unexpected Olympic 800m win, the four world records he has set, nor his dramatic rivalry with Sebastian Coe. For Ovett's actions on the Tartan running tracks of Europe have created an image just as striking as the mysterious one he adopted for so long in private.

He has built an air of invincibility around himself; a Muhammad Ali-like aura which has helped to give him a psychological 'edge' over so many of his fellow competitors. His coach Harry Wilson describes, and indeed regards, him as a 'genius' and sees his unorthodox approach to top class sport as a positive asset. 'He relies very much on his feelings,' Wilson told the late James Coote in an article for the *Sunday Telegraph Magazine*. 'The 1500m is very much a race where feelings are vital. The world of athletics finds it difficult to accept someone completely different from anyone who has gone before.'

From the moment Ovett's rift with the Press developed

in 1975 Wilson, and perhaps Ovett himself, seemed determined to perpetuate the public image of Ovett as an unorthodox and untouchable sporting genius. But now that his track career has reached a temporary lull, Ovett has set about the destruction of his media image and the real Steve Ovett is beginning to emerge in the public eye for the first time.

'The media image was beginning to get out of hand,' explained Ovett in the *TV Times* in September 1982. 'At first the image was deliberate. I knew I was going to be successful, and for quite a long time, and I had seen what happened to George Best and Dave Bedford. They were taken up by the media, made into stars and then after a while the Press got bored with them and started being destructive.

'I was determined that wasn't going to happen to me, so I tried not to get involved at all, but they wrote destructive things anyway. It's got to the stage where I'm beginning to come out like a cross between Attila the Hun and Genghis Khan and I wouldn't like kids coming into the sport to think that you have to be mean to get on. I wanted them to see I'm not as evil as I'm made out to be.'

Apart from the dispelling of his nasty image, Ovett's decision to 'open up' has revealed a man capable of describing life as a top sportsman perhaps better than anyone who has gone before him. 'Becoming well known brings its own problems,' he told the *TV Times*. 'I love to race at Crystal Palace because the crowd gives me such a warm feeling, when I walk on to the track the people stand up and clap. It's marvellous, but it's a double-edged sword, it also distracts me and the knowledge that they expect me to win is a burden.'

'I used to think winning was everything,' he added. 'Being injured has made me appreciate the other side of the coin. It takes a great deal of courage to accept that you are not really fit and to go out there and run anyway. You have to swallow your pride, knowing you are going to be beaten, but it's a sport and I don't believe you should take part only when you know you're going to win.'

Yet losing is a relatively new, and perhaps only temporary, experience for Steve Ovett. He is quintessentially a born winner and also, as he once remarked, 'a born runner'. From the very first moment he began to put one leg in front of the other with any degree of velocity it became apparent that he was destined to reach the athletic heights.

'Fate was kind to him, dealing him a hand of five aces,' says Harry Wilson. 'He has the perfect build — broad shoulders and slim hips — lives in the ideal environment, with ideal places to train on his doorstep — the Downs or the seashore — and this amazing ability to find the most difficult training schedules comes easy to him while others have a struggle.'

As James Coote once wrote — 'Had Doctor Frankenstein turned his hand to creating athletes, not monsters, there is little doubt that the summit of his aspirations would have been cast in the mould of Steve Ovett.'

One

Hurdle Race with No Hurdles

The first bend on which Steve Ovett unleashed his awesome sprinting speed was just around the corner from his parents' Brighton home. He was a mere five-year-old at the time, with long, gangling legs protruding awkwardly from his shorts and a thick mop of curly hair. No victory wave or crowd acclaim accompanied his first experimental 'kick', but the opposition was just as fierce as that he was to face on the world's famous running tracks in later years. Even today, Ovett recalls the incident: 'I smashed some kid over the head with a milk bottle, and had to run like hell to get away from his mother.'

Not exactly a laudable debut! But it soon became apparent that young Steve Ovett possessed a unique natural talent: a seemingly effortless ability to run faster than anyone else around him. Ovett himself has admitted in typically banal fashion that what sets him apart from millions of other dedicated runners around the world was quite simply that, 'I was born to run'. And that gift was to be recognised before he was out of short trousers.

Born in Brighton on 9th October 1955, he was the first child of the marriage between marketstall holder Mick Ovett and his pretty teenage bride, Gay, who christened him Steven Michael James. The close-knit Ovett family and his south coast home town were to have a profound effect on his life and his running. As he once commented: 'I've got the ability, the time, the family, the background, the competition. It's almost fate.'

During his early life, Steve's parents devoted a lot of hard work to building up the family's farm produce stall in

Brighton's open air market — a successful venture which was to be a major factor in providing the money needed to enable Steve to pursue a life dedicated to running, without the burden of financial worries. As a result, he spent a large part of his early years with his grandparents and developed a close and lasting bond with his grandfather Albert, who founded the family's business.

These formative years were both happy and settled ones for Steve and the protectiveness of Ovett family life was, as a result, to become a major influence on his life. In later years, outsiders — particularly the Press — were to view the Ovett household as a fortress which only a chosen few were ever allowed to enter. But to Steve, his sister Sue (two years his junior and now manageress of the family's cafe in Preston Park), and his brother Nicky (ten years younger than Steve and a pupil at Varndean Comprehensive School), the family home in Harrington Villas, set in leafy surroundings on Brighton's northerly suburban fringe, has been the perfect refuge from the outside world.

The house, with a mock-Tudor facade, is a large pre-war semi perched on a rolling hill-top above the coastal resort and offers all the privacy and tranquillity residents in the quiet middle class neighbourhood could require. It lies one and a half miles from the market in Marshall's Row, where Mick Ovett puts in a thirteen hour working day, and a little further again from the town's best-known landmarks along the sea front: the elegant regency crescents, the magnificent Royal Pavilion, the winding Palace Pier and decaying West Pier. But the landmarks in the life of Brighton's best known twentieth century resident are neither sign-posted nor obvious.

In due course of time, this may change. A civic memorial may one day mark his birthplace. Should any such actions be taken, however, it is extremely unlikely that they would have the blessing of one of the town's most famous sons. For while many men and women who achieve fame frequently hanker after privacy, Steve Ovett craves and demands that right. And Brighton's cosmopolitan air unquestionably offers him the perfect background into which he could dissolve in almost absolute anonymity. 'When I go into shops and people ask me my name,' says Ovett, 'and I tell them, they say to me "you're not related to that runner are you?" It's good to have my own private life. It's important to me that I stay the way I am.' (*Athletics Weekly*, 1979).

Growing up in Harrington Villas proved a location eminently suitable to nurturing Steve's raw running talent. For less than a hundred yards from the green front door of No. 8 lies Preston Park, and to find a more private public amenity would be difficult indeed. Though a mere fifth of a mile from the heavy traffic flow of the main A23 London to Brighton road, few passers-by would guess that behind the high stone wall and dense screen of trees lies a patch of ground that for over a dozen years was the favourite training ground of a spindly-legged youngster destined to become one of the world's greatest middle distance runners.

Enter and you find a cricket pitch encircled by an asphalt municipal cycle track: the perfect training track, as fate would have it, literally on Steve Ovett's doorstep. Even in the years that followed when the world's TV cameras were trained on his every race, his training sessions aroused no curiosity in the odd pensioner who dozed on the overlooking park benches, arranged around the cricket ground in the style of a Roman amphitheatre.

As for the occasional passers-by exercising their poodles and small terriers, such Brightonians would no more have thought of approaching the lone athlete than of breaking the park's litter by-laws. Imagine a soccer star in Liverpool enjoying a work-out in a public park without attracting an enthusiastic mob of youngsters within minutes! But this is cosmopolitan Brighton, not Merseyside.

Geographical fortune certainly helped Steve Ovett to develop his unprecedented range of running talents, from sprinting to cross country running. Only two miles up the A23 lie the South Downs, and Stanmer Park provides

Ovett with the ideal setting for his distance running work. 'I love running over the Downs and I'll be running over them when I'm finished with top class athletics,' says Steve, 'it's what relaxes me the best.'(*Athletics Weekly*, 1979). To reach those Downs each day he must negotiate some steep hills and this has undoubtedly supplemented his natural strength and stamina. Like any other Brightonian, Ovett has a particular love of the town's seafront: 'When I was getting over glandular fever (in 1974) I started back in training with some mates from the Brighton Surfers Club. We'd run along a really flat part of the promenade to the West Pier, up and down, about nine o'clock at night. Marvellous.'

One of the most humorous attempts to pigeonhole Ovett's character came from the pen of a Finnish journalist who likened him to Pinkie Brown, the ruthless personification of evil created by Graham Greene in *Brighton Rock*, his novel about the pre-war Brighton underworld. Ovett must find such comparisons amusing; but like Greene's boyhood gangster creation, Steve Ovett is 'real Brighton' to the core and the regency town is as much 'his territory' as it was Pinkie's.

He hates being away from Brighton for long. 'It's where I belong,' he says. 'I'm a home loving boy. I don't like to get too far away from all my old training and drinking haunts. This is my part of the world.' (*Jogging*, 1979). Indeed, his roots are so firmly entrenched in the Sussex town that he refused to be swayed by innumerable scholarship offers from American Colleges and for many years he refused to join the European middle distance circuit, saying, 'I simply prefer being in Brighton.'

The Ovett stall has been operating in Brighton market since the turn of the century and the family can claim to be of true Brightonian stock. The family's unusual name means they are descendants of Ofa — a common Anglo Saxon personal name — and their ancestors came from the eastern Brighton suburb of Ovingdean, the valley of Ofa's people. But the Brighton background and environment together with Ovett's massive talent and determination needed to be complemented by the backing of his parents. Wherever he raced there would be a huge family following screaming support for 'their' Steve and, over the years, he has received unbounded support from his father, Mick, and his mother, Gay.

By the time Steve discovered he could shift his legs at a fair velocity, much to the chagrin of the aforementioned chasing mother, the necessity of education offered a less troublesome channel for his natural speed and aggression. Firmly settled into life at Harrington Villas, with the adjacent world of Preston Park and its splendid manor house to explore and expand his imagination, Steve entered Balfour Primary School just around the corner. Makeshift football matches in the playground, with blazers for posts and only a tennis ball or a stone to kick, have been sporting baptisms for most boys and Steve Ovett was no different. Sandy Cromar, his former teacher at Balfour Primary School, vividly remembers keeping an eye on those playground tussles. 'It was obvious right from the start that Steve was very, very fast,' he recalls. 'He would run around like mad in those games and was so much faster than all the other boys that he would run away from them all and score all the goals.'

During these formative school years, in the early 1960s, football, cricket and running became Steve's sporting activities at Balfour. He is still remembered as 'a bright pupil who was particularly adept at Maths and Science and who had no trouble in passing his eleven-plus examination' but it was his natural athletic flair that set him apart from the other boys. And Steve's grandfather, who took a close interest in his sporting development, reckoned that his grandson's long-legged, wiry build best suited him to high-jumping.

Recalls Mr Cromar: 'Albert was very close to Steve and started to coach him when he was nine or ten. Such was Steve's enthusiasm he would come into school an hour early in the morning and practice with some of the other boys. He was also playing football for Brighton primary schools at the time and, although I always imagined he would become a top sportsman, I thought he would be a footballer, not a runner.'

As the edge of competition with other boys became a factor in Steve's athletic progress, he must also have felt that his sporting future lay in football rather than athletics. At the age of ten he failed to win the high-jump at the annual Brighton Primary Schools championships. After 'shedding quite a few tears about that', as one local athletics official recalled, Steve entered his final year at Balfour and found a more successful athletics niche. He won the 100 and 220 yards races at the 1967 championships and prepared for grammar school life with the reputation of being a sprint champion.

Varndean Grammar School is situated in quiet, leafy surroundings within the same grounds as Balfour. Thus much of the upheaval which accompanies a child's transition from junior to senior school was lost on Steve Ovett, who could glance out of the classroom windows to panoramic views of his home town and the English Channel beyond. Even as a sixth form college today, it retains the distinctively microcosmic air of the traditional grammar school world. Teachers are still considered to be 'masters' rather than the 'lecturers' they now are. And the red brick building, with past head prefects' plaques mounted proudly beside the entrance to the plank-floored main hall and outdoor quadrants leading round the classrooms, remains much the same as when Steve Ovett first entered its special world in September 1967.

In sporting terms, Steve spent his first two years doing cross-country and football in the winter and athletics in the summer. In his second year, at the age of thirteen, he started to concentrate on sprinting and thus came under the wing of the school's track specialist Alan Gray. 'He was basically just another 100 metre and 200 metre runner in those days,' recalls Gray, 'there's a boy in every year who's a natural sprinter and Steve was no different. The big breakthrough came later that summer when he moved up to the quarter-mile.'

Steve's father had been a committee member at Brighton and Hove Athletic Club for a few years and, along with his mother Gay, was a knowledgeable athletics fan with sufficient enthusiasm to make a regular 100 mile round trek to watch the major athletics meetings at London's White City Stadium. At first he attempted to satisfy his son's athletic needs by taking him running around Preston Park, but he soon found that he couldn't match his son's pace and, along with Albert, decided to take him down to the local club's track at Withdean Stadium that summer of 1969.

With the benefit of hindsight, there are many who — having known, however fleetingly, an individual who later achieves greatness — claim they recognised the raw talent from the very beginning. But in the case of Steve Ovett it is a matter of record that many people quite clearly *did* immediately see his amazing potential.

'Mick and Albert brought Steve down to the track one night,' remembers the club's team manager at the time, Tony Tilbury. 'They told me he'd done a bit of running at school and had been quite successful. They thought he could be quite a good athlete and wanted him to join the club. I did the standard thing in such cases and asked Steve to run down the back straight with some other boys. He left them standing and immediately you could see that this young lad had natural talent. His style was incredible for a boy of thirteen; he had the same rangy stride he has today and the flicked-back right arm, which nobody has managed to correct.'

So Steve Ovett marked a significant development in his athletic career by paying his five shilling youth's membership fee and joining the 200 other members of Brighton and Hove AC. The Club had been formed three years earlier when the two local clubs, Brighton AC and Hove AC merged together in an attempt to give their athletes a better deal. The positive signs began to appear by the time of the Mexico Olympics in 1968 when the club provided three members of the British team — Chris Carter, Arthur Jones and Andy Todd.

The annals of athletics history are littered with tales of boys who fall by the wayside after an over-eager coach has tried to develop their talent too early. This certainly wasn't the case with Steve Ovett. 'We had to be very careful with him,' says the club's president Reg Hook. 'When you see youngsters with the kind of talent young Steve displayed you think they can go all of the way to the top, but they need to be carefully nurtured. Nine times out of ten they will spend two years in the sport and then drop out, for a variety of basically adolescence-related reasons. You have to try and maintain their interest without pushing them too hard too soon.

'Steve didn't immediately come under the eye of any specific coach. He came down to the club on Tuesday and Thursday evenings, enjoyed himself and did a bit of training. He had a great deal of talent at nearly every event but we didn't want to treat him as a "special case". He was a good high-jumper, long-jumper and sprinter; it was difficult to suggest where he might best channel his talents, so we just let him try all of the events himself and find the one he enjoyed best.'

The 400 metres has long been regarded as the 'killer' track event. Every event has its particular difficulties, but even Britain's best-ever 400 metre runner, David Jenkins, found himself tying up over the last 100 metres because of fatigue and an excess of lactic acid in his tired limbs. It demands the extension of full sprinting speed all of the way and requires extraordinary power and stamina. Ovett's physique and build suited him well to the event and in September 1969 he had his first taste of success at the distance when he missed breaking the UK record for thirteen-year-olds by a mere tenth of a second. Clocking 53.7 seconds, he became the second fastest 400m runner of his age in Britain.

Mick Ovett knew that his son was blessed with a special

talent and wanted him to benefit from the guidance of an expert coach. Tony Tilbury was short of coaches at Brighton and couldn't guarantee Steve individual attention, but he suggested that his brother Barry, who had recently moved 50 miles away to Walton, might be the man he was looking for.

The Tilbury family had been leading lights in Sussex athletics for many years and Barry still travelled to Brighton at weekends. 'I first saw Steve run when I visited the club in October 1969,' says Barry. 'It was noticeable that he was always out in front and wasn't struggling with hard runs, you could tell he was quite special.'

'So when my brother phoned me and asked me if I was prepared to coach this young Ovett lad, I said "yes". We started in early 1970 when I took an afternoon off work to meet his parents in Harrington Villas. As soon as I went through the front door Mick took me to one side and ushered me into a front room. He sat me down and asked me what I thought Steve could eventually achieve.'

'I thought he would go far so I told him I thought Steve had the potential to run in the Olympics. It's all right talking about it in retrospect, but I could honestly see the talent. Mick was a bit taken aback. I think he thought I was getting carried away, but I certainly wasn't.'

His judgement was backed up by the athletics writer in Brighton's *Evening Argus* that November when he saw Ovett win the annual Crawley Road race and announced, 'Here is a truly outstanding prospect. We are going to see a lot more of Ovett in coming years.'

So Barry Tilbury, a 30-year-old production controller in the printing industry, became responsible for grounding Steve Ovett in the basic techniques of athletics. Relying on Mick to supervise Steve's mid-week training sessions, Barry based Steve's schedules on a five day week. 'It was all relatively slow, progressive work interlaced with a fair sprinkling of faster work on track and grass,' says Barry. 'The major problem was the fact that Steve was so fast and talented that he could win races without training, but he was intelligent enough to know that this work would stand him in good stead in the long run.'

'Steve was a little arrogant, but basically shy in those early days,' says Tilbury, but it was at this point — in early 1970 — that Steve's determination and strength of character began to show through. He was a sufficiently talented schoolboy footballer to play for Brighton boys and was inevitably faced with the dilemma of choosing between football and athletics. His Games master John Smith takes up the story.

'I think you would pick up Steve's go-it-alone attitude from this time. He came to see me one day and said "I know you're picking me for the football team and I know I'm good enough, but I don't want to risk ruining my running by getting injured." In a way I admired the mature and forthright manner in which he addressed the situation, but it was unusual for boys to do this in those days ... especially at the age of fourteen. They were expected to play for the school teams if selected and to fulfill a complete Games programme.

'He played on the right wing and scampered up and down the touchline and was certainly a talented footballer and an asset to the team. But in the end he did virtually buck the system and dig his heels in. We reached an agreement to some extent in the end — Steve pointed out that I couldn't make him play football if he didn't want to — but it was certainly the first exception to the rule, I knew of.

'Otherwise, Steve was a fully committed pupil. I must stress that it was never in his nature to buck the system generally. He was in the school choir, a keen philatelist and a member of the Boy's Brigade. I have many fond memories of him, particularly when he played a little Inca in the school's production of *The Royal Hunt of the Sun*. He wore a little black, curly wig, did the bird song, pranced about the stage and was massacred along with all the other little Incas.'

Little Inca Ovett (who was in fact now 5 foot 9 inches and

weighed almost 10 stone) had made his choice early and even at the age of fourteen was determined to reach the top. His attitude began to bear fruit in June 1970 when he reduced his 400m personal best to a staggering time of 51.6 in winning the Sussex schools Junior Boy's title. Tilbury's guidance was paying dividends and helped to earn Steve's passage to his first major test: the 1970 all-England Schools' Championships at Solihull.

The 'English Schools' is an awesome occasion for any young athlete. A few thrive on the Olympic-style procession of heats, semi-finals, and finals, but the vast majority buckle under the pressure of constant herding, and the generally over-powering regimentation. It is the first national yardstick for any young hopeful. Having been the best in their region, they are pitched into battle with the best from all over the country; the physical demands are great, but the supreme test is in overcoming the mental pressures.

Usually those who are suspect in that department fall by the wayside and as Tony Tilbury relates, Steve Ovett — today considered to be the Borg of the track — suffered from the same anxieties as the other youngsters. 'My brother had to be very close to Steve on these occasions because Steve was very nervous and keyed-up. Barry would have to take Steve away from the crowds and calm him down around the back of the stadia. Steve had a fanatical parent following; wherever he ran, there would be at least a dozen relations screaming for him at the tops of their voices. And I can remember Steve once saying to Barry that he wondered whether it was worth carrying on because of the tensions that were put upon him.'

Steve travelled up to the Midlands with the Sussex team, each of whom stayed with an allocated local family, but behind him the Ovett entourage swept in convoy up the M1: his parents, grandparents, brother, sister, aunts, uncles and cousins all made the trip. The pressures on young Steve were enormous, but he clocked a championship record of 51.8 seconds to win the final by fifteen yards. He had passed his first big test with flying colours and gave his family something to celebrate.

Steve's training partner Peter Francis travelled to Solihull along with Barry Tilbury. 'He was on the road to the top from then on,' says Francis, a land manager from Weybridge, Surrey. 'Mrs Ovett was in tears and there was much rejoicing. The whole family had booked into a local motel and we all had a great evening; Mick bought us all a slap-up dinner and we had a right old knees-up. That was the Ovett family: they gave Steve all of the encouragement he could have possibly needed to reach the top.' Recognition tempered by caution was the reaction in the *Brighton and Hove Herald*. Athletics columnist Alan Buchanan described Steve as 'an excellent prospect for the future and could go right to the top of the tree, but he will now find people setting him apart as an individual and expecting the best from him every time out'.

But Barry Tilbury was far from content to let Steve rest on his laurels. He had brought him together with another young runner, Peter Francis, and one result of their friendship was an attempt to push Steve through the two minute barrier for 800m. The two runners stayed at each other's homes for long weekends and became close, but the main object of their partnership was to take Steve another step up the athletics ladder. Tom Byers shocked the whole athletics world by out-pacing Ovett in a world record attempt in 1981, but it wasn't the first time such plans had back-fired on Steve.

Peter Francis was, in fact, his first 'hare'. 'I was older and stronger than Steve and blessed with a fair turn of speed,' remarks Francis. 'The problem was that I'd go off, judge the pace well and Steve would catch me and I'd out-sprint him or I'd go off fast and he'd never manage to catch me. The irony was that we ran 2 minutes 0.0 seconds, but never managed to crack two minutes.' Nevertheless, Steve Ovett had completed a more than satisfactory first track season under Barry Tilbury's wing. (His 100m and 200m personal bests of 11.8 and 23.8 seconds ranked him alongside the country's best sprinters of his age and he had also long-jumped 20 feet 6 inches and clocked 4:10.7 in his first 1500m race; so he was quite an all-round athlete.)

But despite his great sporting talents, life wasn't all serious training and racing, as Peter Francis recalls. 'When I went down to Steve's at weekends we would go out for meals, go ten-pin bowling or go to discos. I can remember more than one time he would end up with my girlfriend: he certainly knew how to turn on the charm. But the main thing that sticks in my mind was the fact that he was a lazy bloke. We'd go out running over the Downs in a foot of snow sometimes, but he wasn't particularly keen on training and preferred to stay in bed most of the time. Everyone would get up at about seven o'clock on a Saturday morning but Steve wouldn't get out of bed until one o'clock in the afternoon.'

Through the winter of 1970–71 Barry Tilbury carefully planned Steve's training and, in due course, 'sleepy Steve' began to display talent at cross-country and road running. He finished second in the Sussex Boys' cross-country championships at Stanmer Park, third in the Sussex schools' event and returned to the track in early 1971 as a much stronger athlete. As early as May, he smashed through the two minutes barrier for 800 metres by clocking 1:56.8 in finishing second to a boy four years his senior in a race at Withdean.

Influenza and injury combined to make June 1971 one of the most disappointing months in Ovett's career. After collecting the Sussex Youths 400m and 800m titles, he managed only fifth place over two laps in the Southern Youths championships and such were the standards he and Barry were working to that they were disappointed with his third placing against older boys in the English schools' 400m (in a time of 50.4). To some observers Ovett's career appeared to be levelling out; in their eyes the physical advantage he had held over other youths was beginning to disappear. He answered the critics in the best possible way: by running 49.8, an incredible time for a fifteen-year-old, in winning the AAA Youths 400m title at Wolverhampton. Passing 200m in the lightning fast time of 23.5 seconds, Ovett proved he was the best fifteen- or sixteen-year-old quarter-miler in Britain by finishing well ahead of the rest of the field.

'I was never surprised at anything Steve achieved,' says Barry Tilbury, 'He was always yards faster than other lads he came up against. He had a superman type of air around him even then. You always felt he could change up a gear if he needed, he's always seemed to have a lot in reserve.'

Ovett appeared to be slotting back snugly into the 400m, but he ended the season by smashing the UK 800m record for fifteen-year-olds at Crystal Palace in only his third serious two-lap race. His time of 1:55.3 didn't surprise Barry Tilbury, but that wasn't the case with the athlete himself. 'I was very surprised,' said Steve, who put in his crucial burst with 200m left, a feature which was to become the hallmark of his racing tactics. But even fifteen-year-old Steve Ovett was essentially a racer. 'I just wanted to win a tough invitation race,' he said. 'The record came as an unexpected but welcome bonus.'

Steve Ovett was well and truly treading the precarious path which leads to the top of the athletics tree. As his club President Reg Hook put it, 'he was progressing as if he were in a hurdles race with no hurdles'. He had completed another successful season, but everything in the garden of the Ovett's home wasn't rosy.

At the beginning of October 1971 the following letter landed on the doormat of 8 Harrington Villas:

> 'Dear Michael,
>
> Your increased involvement at club level has brought about a set of circumstances that apparently prevents you from divorcing Steve's training and racing programme from your club loyalty...
> I think I'm in the best position to judge what races he needs ... the boy is only sixteen and needs a careful progressive build up each winter ... I fully understand your reaction when you found that after making all the decisions for Steve over a period of fifteen years you now have little say in his running

career, but if you want me to coach him to the best of my ability you must have faith in me. Living over 50 miles away means I have to rely very heavily on you to carry through Steve's coaching programme to completion. I think you will agree that the results so far indicate that we are on the right track.

Yours etc., Barry Tilbury.

'Mick and Gay took the letter very hard,' recalls Barry. 'And within five or six weeks we had parted company. I told them at the outset that I didn't want parental interference to be a problem and they assured me that it wouldn't, but Mick became more involved at the club and a split became inevitable. I spoke to Gay on the phone after I'd sent the letter and she said "what we don't like is the fact that you're trying to turn Steve into something he'll never be ... a 1500m runner." Ironic, isn't it? He's only the world record holder!'

Steve's split from Barry Tilbury was observed from an unbiased vantage point by Peter Francis. 'How the Tilburys and Ovetts got together in the first place I'll never know. They're both forceful, outgoing families and could only ever repel each other like two positive magnets. But Barry undoubtedly played a vital role in Steve's development. His talent was obvious, but he needed Barry to guide him through these initial years in athletics and to keep his interest in the sport until he developed the strength and maturity to propel himself to the top. Barry took Steve to the stage where he needed a mentor rather than a coach, and to do that by the age of fifteen going on sixteen was pretty unique.'

The result of the split was that Steve lost a talented coach and, with the help of his father, spent sixteen months coaching himself. And in his first interview in *Athletics Weekly*, Steve talked about his training philosophies: 'I think all young athletes need some form of guidance and encouragement when they first take up athletics. But they should not become dependent on their coaches to make major decisions. I strongly believe that athletes should be able to think and decide for themselves.' But, honest as ever, he admitted in the same interview, that 'having a family totally immersed in athletics can have its drawbacks'.

In March 1972 Steve came up against a young runner who had been developing under the strong influence of his father, who reckoned his fragile-looking son was eventually capable of running three seconds faster than the then world record for the 1500m. Ovett finished second in the English schools cross-country championships, run over four gruelling miles of Hillingdon mud — a remarkable achievement for a young runner who topped the UK rankings in a sprint event.

Eight places and twenty-three seconds behind Ovett, trailed home a skinny Yorkshire lad who had been carefully nurtured on his father's tough training schedules. The next time they met, six and a half years later in Prague, the stage would be infinitely more salubrious and the result a great deal closer. Between them would be wedged the most burning question in sporting history since the Ali–Frazier era in boxing. His name was, of course, Sebastian Coe.

Nothing stimulates athletes of all ages and capabilities quite like the excitement of an Olympic year. And Steve Ovett, probably unaware of the lad who finished well behind him at Hillingdon and the fact that eight years later they would take part in the most eagerly awaited foot-running confrontation in Olympic history, trained hard for the 1972 track season.

According to Barry Tilbury a typical week's training for Steve Ovett that winter would read as follows:

Monday – 30 minutes fartlek (a long run punctuated by short bursts of sprinting.

Tuesday – 4 × 150m fast. 10 minutes recovery. 4 × 150m fast.

Wednesday – 30 minutes fartlek

Thursday – 3 × 300m fast. 10 minutes recovery. 3 × 300m fast.

Friday – Rest.

Saturday – Race
Sunday – 4 miles easy run.

That tough schedule paid dividends when Steve made his first major impression on senior athletics in April. At the Newham Games, the traditional pipe-opener to the Southern athletics season, he stuck to the slip-stream of international quarter-miler Martin Winbolt-Lewis to defeat several international runners in a 600m race. His second placed time of 79.5 seconds was an astonishing performance for a sixteen-year-old and only Geoff Capes' equalling of the UK shot-putt record was mentioned ahead of it in the meeting reports.

Steve Ovett had 'arrived'. He had lived up to that well-worn cliché which in athletics means you have successfully bridged the gap between junior (aged seventeen to twenty) and senior competition — a gap which many promising athletes have failed to cross. The amazing thing was that Steve Ovett had done it at the age of sixteen. As Reg Hook points out: 'Steve never encountered the problems of stepping from junior to senior athletics. When he became a junior he was better than the top athletes in Britain and even as a youth he was in effect a mature senior athlete.'

June 1972 was a significant month in the life of Steve Ovett. He set a UK sixteen-year-olds 800m record of 1:53.3 in the Sussex County Championships and then reduced it to 1:52.2 in the county schools' event two weeks later. Steve's grandfather was as proud as punch witnessing his grandson's masterful victory, by the length of the home-straight, at Withdean Stadium. Still very close to Steve, he had recently bought a flat close to the track especially to see him run more often. That day must have remained in Steve's mind ever since, for Albert tragically collapsed in the stand and died of a heart-attack.

'It really upset Steve,' remembers Barry Tilbury, 'because they were so close: they were more like pals than grandfather and grandson. Albert started Steve's athletic career rolling and he would have done anything for him. If he needed a new pair of running spikes he would go straight out and buy them.' Coming on top of his athletic commitments and in the middle of his 'O' level exams, it was a crushing blow. But Steve Ovett ended the season in style by winning the English Schools' Intermediate 800m title and retaining his AAA Youths 400m title in 49.1, having reduced his personal best for the one-lap distance to 48.4 which ranked him 30th on the UK senior men's lists.

As one great influence on Steve's life sadly faded into the background another emerged in the shape of Harold Wilson. Not the Leader of the Opposition, but an outgoing Welshman: Harry Wilson, one of Britain's premier middle distance coaches.

The two met by chance on a coaching course at Crystal Palace in early 1973. Steve was to say of him in later years, 'Harry's temperament and attitude towards things are so similar to mine that it was almost as if we were destined to meet' (*Athletics Weekly*, 1979). In turn, Wilson immediately noted 'a remarkable maturity for one so young'. But that wasn't all he noted. 'Steve wanted to join my group of distance runners because the sprinters he was working with were not extending him much. Well, he left the distance runners standing in a session of uphill running and it was obvious that here was a real talent.'

If Wilson's view needed reinforcing, Welsh international distance runner Fred Bell was also impressed. 'Here was this skinny kid who came along from the sprint group to join us for an interval session over a 1000m course,' he recalled in *Jogging*. 'I was super fit at the time and immediately went to the front. Suddenly there was this kid, running alongside me, looking very comfortable with easy, relaxed, flowing stride! I tried to drop him on the hills but he'd just pull me back by the top of each one. We left the others way behind and he stayed with me all the way. Later I found out he was a 400m runner from Brighton called Ovett. I said to Harry, "That kid is not just good. He's going to be great."'

'A monkey could have coached Steve Ovett,' was the view of one Brighton athletics writer and represented the general feeling among the town's athletics fraternity which knew his talent so well. 'Ovett would have reached the top in any case and it was obvious that the monkey would be applauded as the world's greatest coach.' Such a view was unfair to the sometimes underestimated role played by Harry Wilson in taking Steve Ovett to the very pinnacle of the athletics success. Experience at senior level and a knowledgeable mentor who could help him develop his full potential were what Steve most needed.

There is another side to the argument. As Wilson related in an *Athletics Weekly* interview six years later: 'I remember when I first started coaching Steve a very well known coach, who shall remain nameless, said to me: "I think you're a brave fellow. That lads got so much talent I'd be afraid to coach him in case it went wrong." Well its nice to think that it hasn't gone wrong and that you've played your part.'

After Steve finished a remarkable second in the English Schools cross-country championships, Wilson proceeded to provide Ovett with the second part of that critical combination in helping Steve to break through on to the senior international scene during the summer of 1973. His season opened on a high note in May with a convincing victory over Britain's number two 800m runner Pete Browne in a 600m race at the Newham Floodlit meeting, followed by a defeat of international club-mate Peter Standing in notching a personal best of 3:53.4 in collecting the 1500m title at the Sussex Senior Championships. Later in the month he gave further evidence of his extraordinary range of talents by clocking a 400m personal best of 48.0 when finishing a creditable sixth in the Inter-Counties Championships — less than half a second behind Olympic 400m hurdles bronze medallist John Sherwood.

The Southern Junior Championships at Crystal Palace on 17th June 1973 staged the curtain raiser of a double feature which has caused athletics fans from all over Britain to turn up in their droves at the home of British athletics ever since. Unleashing a fearsome 'kick' around the final bend to win the metric mile title, Ovett was reported in *Athletics Weekly* as 'gesturing extravagantly to the crowd to show how easy 3:51.6 is'.

Seven days later he returned to the same track for the Southern Senior Championships and shattered all previous records set by seventeen and eighteen-year-olds over 800m by clocking an amazing time of 1:48.4 when he only just failed to head off the challenge of Pete Browne after a neck-and-neck duel up the home straight. Both Steve's time and his performance rocked the British athletics scene. Ovett had proved he could match such a renowned battler as Browne as well as defeating international half-miler Colin Campbell. Some kind of break-through was expected from the lanky, grimacing Brighton runner but nobody had anticipated the degree seventeen-year-old Ovett was capable of imprinting himself on the British senior athletics scene.

Steve's initial reaction was: 'I was disappointed at losing, but pleased with the time. I knew I was ready to run less than 1 minute 50 seconds, but how much under depended on the pace.' So, in mid-July 1973 the A level art, maths and physics student had hoisted himself to eighth place in the UK 800m ranking lists. And, after overcoming the effects of an ankle injury, prepared himself for his debut in the Amateur Athletic Association Championships, which have served as the unofficial British Championships since 1880.

The mustachioed figure of Dave Bedford, following his breathtaking and world record breaking 1971 season and disappointing Olympic season, was still the king of British athletics. His outspoken and debonair character had been responsible for a resurgence of interest in the sport and he added further fuel to the flickering flames by winning the 10,000m in the world record time of 27:30.8. He dominated the show, milking the applause from the crowd and giving a distinct victory sign (the Harvey Smith variety) to the

Crystal Palace press-box while rumours were rife that he would be joining the frowned-upon professional athletics circus.

Ovett was destined to take over his mantle as king of the Crystal Palace crowd and fierce enemy of the press-box, but in 1972 he was very much the novice thrown in at the deep end as he faced Britain's number one 800m runner Andy Carter together with a handful of top foreign runners. On the Friday night of the two-day meeting he qualified for the final by chasing America's Mark Winzenreid all of the way home to create his first world record, an age-seventeen best of 1:47.5.

The Saturday afternoon final turned out to be a classic two-lap race, widely acknowledged to be the finest 800m race ever held in Britain. Winzenreid blazed around the first lap in 51 seconds to set up Andy Carter for a new UK national and UK all-comers record of 1:45.1. Ovett finished sixth in a new personal best of 1:47.3 with Carter and Browne the only Britons ahead of him. And with three places being up for grabs in January 1974's Commonwealth Games, Ovett was no longer regarded as 'that skinny 400m runner from Brighton'.

But defeat came his way in the City Mile at Motspur Park on 25th July, when he finished nearly two seconds behind Bristol runner Nick Rose. It was Ovett, once again, however, who stole the headlines. In his first ever mile race he had set a UK junior record with a time of four minutes exactly. Passing the 1500m mark in a personal best time of 3:44.8, Ovett was more than three seconds behind Rose but he drove hard around the last bend and passed four men in the straight to gain second place.

It was yet another important breakthrough for Steve. The doors were now open for future success in the 'blue riband' event of athletics. Mick Ovett, however, was far from happy. 'I was feeling quite pleased with myself,' said Steve, 'but my dad said "what a bloody awful race that was". In fact I'd run the last lap in about 55 seconds, much faster than anybody else, but still lost the race. I'd misjudged it, so he was quite right.' Standards had certainly changed considerably since Roger Bannister's almighty effort to break the four minute barrier nineteen years earlier. Here was a seventeen-year-old schoolboy running four minutes dead in his mile debut and declaring afterwards, 'I wasn't surprised at the time, but I ran like an absolute idiot.'

At the beginning of August he finished third over 800m in his senior international debut for Britain in a match against France in Sotteville. Then it was on to the West German town of Duisburg for the first acid test of Steve's progress. The European Junior Championships combine the demanding format of tough heats, semi-finals and finals with the matching together of Europe's pretenders to the 'athletics greats' crowns for the first time.

The spirits of the British contingent were raised on the opening day when Birmingham's black sprinter Sonia Lannaman won the 100m and Ovett's training partner Lesley Keirnan, with whom he was becoming increasingly more friendly, took second place in the women's 800m. Ovett, himself, found the pressures of coping with the role of clear favourite for the men's 800m slightly over-bearing, but nevertheless dealt with the heats and semi-finals very calmly.

The troll-like figure of West Germany's Willi Wulbeck attempted to draw the sting out of Ovett's sprint finish by going off fast in the final to lead in a time of 52.6 at halfway with Ovett down in fifth place. Gathering his strength down the back straight, Ovett was within five metres of Wulbeck as they entered the last 100m. Wulbeck must have been fatigued out in front, but, with his home crowd roaring towards the tape, he wasn't going to relinquish his grasp on the gold medal without a fight. Steve appeared to have held back his 'kick' for too long but with a desperate lunge he hit the tape a stride ahead of Wulbeck to win by a mere four-hundredth of a second (in a time of 1:47.53).

With the Ovett family 'fan club' taking a rest in Spain, Steve could feel pleased with himself on two counts. He had coped with the role of favourite in a major championship and had judged the race to perfection. He would be seeing a lot more of Wulbeck and the tall Belgian Ivo Van Damme who finished fourth, but his immediate reaction to the tight final was one of relief at finishing ahead of them. 'I intended to win it with a late "kick",' he said. 'But I couldn't have left it any later. Still, it made an exciting race.

'I certainly never intended them getting that far away. But that's my trouble, I'm lazy. I like running from behind because of my fast finish. But you live and learn. I'll be more careful another time.'

As Ovett related to Dave Cocksedge in *Athletics Weekly*, the general experience of the championships was just as important as the competition. 'Duisburg was a big success for me because I had a good time socially as well. The accommodation wasn't so good — some of us were sleeping two to a bed — but the atmosphere and the team spirit was just tremendous. I really enjoyed it. I'm lucky enough to have a great coach in Harry Wilson: there just wasn't another thing he could have done to prepare Lesley and me for our races out there. And we came back with a gold and a silver medal to show for it.'

In less than ten months, Wilson had taken Ovett from being potentially Britain's greatest ever young running talent to being a seventeen-year-old wonder-kid with senior experience and international honours to his credit. And after suffering an adverse reaction in finishing a disappointing ninth in the mile at the end-of-season International Athletes Club/Coca Cola meeting at Crystal Palace he was faced with the chance of clinching a Commonwealth Games place at the English trials meeting.

The 800m was the event which posed the selectors the biggest headache. Andy Carter was already assured of one of the three places with Pete Browne almost certain to fill the second berth. The best of the rest therefore lined up at Crystal Palace on a chilly October afternoon to do battle for the remaining place. Such a run-off situation was never likely to suit Ovett, who was suffering from the effects of a longer and more tiring season than the other runners, and in a dramatic race he managed only third place. Jersey athlete Colin Campbell caused a minor surprise by winning, four tenths of a second ahead of Ovett, with the unfancied nineteen-year-old Tony Settle from Sale in Cheshire taking second place.

But the selectors had declared before the trials that past performances would be taken into consideration and they were faced with an agonising choice between Ovett and Campbell. Steve's Duisburg win proved he could handle the major championships situation of three tough races within a short space of time and the fact that he had beaten Campbell, when both were feeling fresh, in the Southern Championships at the start of the season seemed to swing the verdict heavily in his favour. The selection committee, however, felt that Ovett, now eighteen, would have plenty of opportunities to run in future major championships and plumped for the more experienced Campbell, giving the official excuse for his omission as the fact that he should be sitting his A level 'mock' examinations while the Games were taking place.

Steve's father and Harry Wilson expressed amazement at the decision and prompted a flood of letters supporting the case for Steve's selection to *Athletics Weekly*. Ovett had suffered his first brush with the athletics administration and was bitterly disappointed, but he significantly made the most of it. His resolve to succeed at senior international level hardened considerably and was to create a remarkable reaction later in 1974. He promised to become so good that the selectors wouldn't dare leave him out again.

'I'd be lying if I said I wasn't bitter,' he told Dave Cocksedge. 'I felt I had proved I could rise to the big occasion, but I'll tell you one thing. This business has made me more determined now, so maybe the experience has been good for me in that sense. That's never going to happen to me again — I'm gonna get out there and run and run and run.'

Running had progressively enveloped Steve Ovett's life. He had glided through the problems of adolescence and the struggles for influence on his career as if they hadn't been there, until, at the tender age of eighteen, the world of athletics lay at his feet. Nothing could put the brakes on his meteoric rise to the top — 'It was as if he was in a hurdles race with no hurdles.'

Two

Just the Best in Britain

Throughout the winter of 1973–74 Steve Ovett fought a lonely war with himself, pounding the undulating backstreets of Brighton and Hove with the disappointment of missing out on a trip to the Commonwealth Games weighing heavily on his mind.

The winter nights must have seemed even longer to Steve when he contracted glandular fever just before Christmas. The ailment is feared by young athletes and was already in the process of cutting short the promising career of Steve's friend and training partner Peter Francis. The loss of three months' training was therefore not such a high price for Steve to pay, but his plans to make the Commonwealth Games selectors regret their decision by taking the international athletics scene by storm in the Rome European Championships seemed to have disappeared.

After making a complete recovery by Easter, Harry Wilson took an unfit and mentally despondent Steve Ovett to the Welsh coastal town of Merthyr Mawr to find out whether anything could be salvaged from his apparently submerged summer track season. After a weekend of relaxation, Wilson led Steve to the foot of a giant sandhill, known in athletics circles as 'the Big Dipper', and asked him to run to the top. 'Somehow I got to the top,' recalled Steve in a *Sunday Times* article. 'That one big effort was the difference between me going to Rome and doing nothing all summer.'

A platform was soon built for the track season and the effort was to prove a significant turning point in Ovett's running career. The immediate effects soon became apparent when he put on his spiked running shoes for his first major race of what should have been a 'lost' season. In collecting his first senior championship title, Steve reversed the one–two placings from the previous year's Southern Championships 800m final, in June, by holding off Pete Browne's home-straight challenge.

That impressive performance, in which Ovett also defeated Colin Campbell, intensified the build up to the AAA Championships and his confrontation with Andy Carter to decide who was Britain's undisputed number one 800m runner. Carter had been Britain's best two-lapper for three years and looked in little danger of relinquishing his position, but suddenly the precocious European Junior Champion from Brighton presented himself as a 'handful', to say the least.

After only 200 metres Ovett thought he had 'well and truly blown it' as he found himself well out of contention in next to last place with America's Mark Winzenreid, Jamaica's Byron Dyce and Carter battling for the lead. A lap further on, with just a furlong remaining, he was still in seventh place, twelve metres behind Winzenreid. But Ovett changed up a gear as he rounded the final turn to treat the Crystal Palace crowd to a sight which has since become the major attraction at the stadium. Producing a finishing surge as devastating as the one which won the 1972 Olympic final for Dave Wottle, he flashed past the leaders to breast the tape a tenth of a second ahead of Carter in a personal best time of 1 minute 46.9 seconds.

The exploits of David Bedford, Brendan Foster, Alan Pascoe and David Jenkins had prompted a resurgence in British athletics throughout the early seventies but at last a 'golden boy', capable of beating the rest of the world, had been 'found'. This feeling was reinforced when Ovett became the youngest ever sub-four minute miler in a race he had described as a 'training run'. Following successive laps of 60.2, 61.1 and 63.0, Ovett blazed around the final circuit of the Brigg Mile at Haringy to clock 3:59.4 — an astounding performance for an eighteen-year-old 800m runner.

800 metre running was still Ovett's forte, however, and by defeating 1969 European silver medallist Jozef Plachy and Carter once again in the UK/Czechoslovakia match in Edinburgh he staked his claims for being a medal contender in Rome. Carter had been comprehensively knocked from his perch. 'Not only that,' said the *Stretford Harrier*, 'he even won the sweepstake.' Ovett's prediction of five minutes and fourteen seconds was the most accurate among the British team in estimating the duration of BAAB Chairman Harold Abrahams' after-dinner speech.

Nevertheless, Carter gained revenge in a 1000m race at Gateshead and Ovett suffered a further defeat in the Emsley Carr Mile before it was announced that he and David McMeekin were to be Britain's 800m representatives in the European Championships. Carter was also selected, but injury prevented him from turning out in the Italian capital. The two defeats had brought a halt to Ovett's trail-blazing season and suggested that the effects of losing three months' basic winter training had finally caught up with him. Harry Wilson's answer was to take Ovett back to Merthyr Mawr 'to rediscover myself', as Ovett commented, before the British team flew out to Rome. A weekend of relaxed training on the beach worked wonders.

On the opening day of a memorable championship for British athletics, McMeekin was eliminated in the heats and Ovett comfortably qualified for the semi-finals by finishing second in his heat. British hopes of 800m glory now rested solely on his shoulders and Ovett responded by producing a masterly display to qualify for the final. Moving from fourth to first place over the last 200m, Ovett pipped one of the favourites, Luciano Susanj of Yugoslavia, to win his semi-final by one-tenth of a second (1:47.1 to 1:47.2).

Suddenly Ovett became one of the favourites, along with Susanj and Marcello Fiasconaro, a Springbok of Italian parentage. Susanj had prepared thoroughly for the championships by training at altitude and running several 'sharpening' races against the tough Kenyan Mike Boit and the USA's number one, Rick Wohlhuter, in order to bring his performances to a peak in Rome. But the fact that Fiasconaro had broken Dave Wottle's world 800m record by 0.6 of a second (1:43.7) in Milan the previous year made him the clear favourite.

With the crowd roaring him on, 'Fiasc' bowed to the pampering of the masses and thus blew his chances. He stormed around the first lap in the suicidal time of 50.1 with Ovett nearly one and a half seconds behind in fifth place. The 600m is traditionally the make or break point in an 800m race and Fiasconaro was still a good 4 metres clear of Deiter Fromm, but in a split second the race was transformed.

Susanj unleashed a fearsome kick to shoot from fourth to first place, opening up an unassailable lead as he sped around the final bend. The speed with which he executed his attack stunned the rest of the field and Ovett in particular, finding himself hopelessly boxed in, was powerless to respond. But, as the chasing pack unfurled into the home straight, Ovett sprinted from fifth to second place — thus passing through the gap which separates senior international 'respectability' from the domain of the world beaters. He reached the silver medal position 25m from the tape with Susanj some 15m clear. The Yugoslav collected the gold medal with a winning time of 1:44.07, while Ovett surpassed all expectations by taking the silver in a European Junior Record of 1:45.8.

The reaction from the sportswriters and athletics fraternity was typified by *Athletics Weekly* editor Mel Watman, who wrote: 'He is the greatest young middle distance talent I have laid eyes on since the Jim Ryun of a decade ago.' Ovett's reaction, however, shocked many people and laid the foundations for his future battles with the Press.

'It wasn't a good run,' Ovett said at the post-race press conference. 'I know I did 1 minute 45.8 seconds and got a silver medal but a silver doesn't glitter like a gold does. If I could have broken at 300m I think I could have won, but there was no way out for me at that point. I was blocked in and when I did get a clear run at Susanj it was too late. I've learned my lesson though.'

After reflecting on the experience, Ovett told Dave Cocksedge, 'It took me the whole of the last bend to pull myself out of that "Oh Christ, there goes my gold medal" feeling and get back into the race. I was so disgusted with myself that the feeling carried over to the press conference later and stayed with me all evening. I'm afraid I was a bit abrupt with the British Press boys. But at the time I just wanted to see my parents and talk the race over with Harry then go away, alone, and work out my feelings.'

It was a similar reaction to that of Lynn Davies when, as the defending champion at the 1968 Olympics, Bob Beamon's incredible long jump of 8.90m depressed him to such an extent that he couldn't motivate himself enough to fight for the 'minor' medals. The truth was that British athletes were expected to be satisfied with silver and bronze medals.

Ovett's dissatisfaction with a silver medal was a firm indication that he was well on the way towards becoming a world beater. He explained his attitude to Cocksedge: 'I know I could have done a lot better. I felt I'd let a lot of people down — my family and Harry. I've never yet run a race that satisfied me totally. I suppose that's one of the things that keeps me going: a sort of striving for perfection. I know you have to accept that you can't win all of the time in this game, but in every specific race situation I'm in, I'm there to break the tape ahead of the others — or what's the point of it all? Though we all finished within a couple of metres in that scramble for the silver medal, it wasn't a great field that Susanj absolutely urinated on.'

Steve Ovett was an eighteen-year-old with high standards and dynamic self-motivation. But five years later, when Mel Watman asked him if he had changed since being so bitterly disappointed with his Rome performance, it was clear that he had mellowed somewhat. 'Yes, I have changed,' he replied. 'It was a necessary stage to go through, I had to be like that to start with. Every kid is like that, obsessed with achieving certain things, but I think you appreciate your situation a little better with time. You have different standards.'

Nevertheless, Ovett's silver medal prompted most observers into talking about him as a medal contender for the 1976 Olympics. His drive to reach the top of world athletics was accelerating rapidly. But when he returned home, Steve had to sort out his future, in the light of having passed A level Art, but having failed Maths and Physics. More than forty tempting scholarship offers from American colleges were carefully considered, but Steve's attachment to Brighton was so great that even thoughts of studying at Loughborough were eventually overcome as he enrolled on a Business Administration and Photographic Art course at Brighton College of Art and Design.

Cultivating a caricatured art student image by growing a goatee beard, Steve's running career took a further step in the right direction in the winter months. He had always struggled with the heavy training schedules he needed to perform to compete with the world's best middle distance runners; lonely and monotonous work at the best of times. But at the beginning of 1975 he began training every day with his club-mate Matt Paterson, a local schoolmaster. The forging of their relationship, suggested by Brighton and Hove AC's team manager Tony Tilbury in an attempt to bring Ovett closer to the club, was to prove significant in his running career.

As early as March 1975 it was becoming clear that his 'shared' workload was paying dividends. For Ovett won the National Junior Cross Country title at Luton by a record margin of 35 seconds. Now turned nineteen, he had proved that he was the best British runner of his age over six miles of mud as well as being one of the world's leading 800m runners.

Steve Ovett was building up a fearsome reputation in

athletic circles and the 1975 track season presented itself as a test of how much he could consolidate from his international breakthrough of the previous year. With the Olympic Games looming on the horizon just twelve months away much was expected of him — especially in Britain's fight to improve their dismal Europa Cup record.

A record two-day British crowd of 22,000 saw the British men's team enjoy one of its finest hours by finishing ahead of Poland and the USSR in the Europa Cup semi-final at Crystal Palace in July. Ovett ran his first confident major race of the season to win the 800m in 1:46.7. After applauding the crowd for their support — thousands had to be turned away — Ovett ascended the main stand steps for one of the most remarkable press conferences in British sporting history.

Asked if he was looking forward to running in the Europa Cup final in Nice, Ovett told reporters that he would not be there as he planned to end his season with a run in the AAA Championships in order to start his preparations for the Montreal Olympics. 'My athletics programme is dominated by next year's Olympics and the Europa Cup final does not fit into my plans,' said Ovett. 'That weekend I plan to hitch-hike to Athens to watch my girlfriend Lesley Keirnan in the European Junior Championships.'

More than one athletic writer professed their amazement at this decision and his apparent lack of patriotism. Heated words were exchanged. Finally Ovett picked up the nearest chair, placed it in the centre of the room and told the goggle-eyed reporters that if they weren't satisfied with his answers they could interview the chair and invent answers they would find acceptable. He then stormed out of the door, vowing never to return again. And he hasn't.

Ovett's decision not to run in Nice drew immediate scorn from his fellow-competitors, the Press and the athletics authorities. Brendan Foster commented: 'Of course Ovett is right and the Olympics are the most important thing but you have to step up to it. You can't miss out rungs of the ladder up to the Olympics.' David Jenkins was incensed, asking the rhetorical question of why the other runners had bothered to 'torture themselves' to qualify.

A major sporting controversy erupted. The Press branded Ovett as 'arrogant', 'immature' and 'unpatriotic', while he agreed to be interviewed on BBC radio to put forward his point of view. 'Unless I can run in a race where I can get the best out of myself, it would be a snub to my country,' maintained Ovett. 'There is no more nationalistic runner than myself. If you had been at Crystal Palace you would have seen my family waving a six foot six Union Jack.'

Harry Wilson further developed Steve's point of view in the correspondence columns of *Athletics Weekly*: 'I agree that Steve is privileged to run for Great Britain but if he's the best in the country then it's his right to compete or not. If any athlete is the number one in a country then surely he has earned the right to be selected — his selection isn't a favour that has to be granted. What I must stress is that he has the right to say what he thinks regardless of whether everyone agrees with what he says.'

The whole controversy was focused on the question of whether athletes — individuals in an amateur sport — should have the right to control their own careers. Six years later, Ovett and Allan Wells were still battling for the 'moral' victory of having the freedom to choose where they wanted to run. But in 1975, the pressure caused Ovett to relent and inform the selectors that he would be prepared to run after all.

With storms blowing over, Ovett prepared for the Nice meeting by once again displaying his amazing range of talents. He clocked 21.7 for 200m (many people maintain it should have been 22.7) and 48.7 for 400m in a league match at Barking. At the beginning of August, he retained his AAA Championships' 800m title by finishing a stride ahead of Pete Browne after the two adversaries had fought a bruising battle for two laps.

Ovett was far from happy with his performance. 'I'm not running well,' he said '— only just the best in Britain.'

The Europa Cup Final proved to be a great success for British athletics. Victories by David Jenkins (400m), Alan Pascoe (400m hurdles), Geoff Capes (shot) and the men's 4×400m relay team capped by a crushing win by Brendan Foster in the 5,000m. And, after what had been a disappointing season in light of his remarkable 1974 season, Ovett brought a resoundingly successful conclusion to a controversial chapter in his career with a resounding win in the 800m.

Less than 100 per cent fit and with controversial build-up still on his mind, Ovett had feared losing against men he would normally be expected to beat and thus starting his vital pre-Olympic winter training with a psychological disadvantage. Such fears were swept aside as he demolished the field in a manner similar to the way in which Susanj had won the European title twelve months earlier.

The arms started flying as a cluster of runners gathered themselves for a last assault at the 600m mark. Caught in the thick of it, Ovett saw an opening and moved into top gear. A five metre gap immediately opened up and Steve maintained his form through the tape, finishing eight metres clear of Deiter Fromm in a time of 1:46.6.

The Nice thing was blown out of all proportion by the Press,' claimed Ovett in *Athletics Weekly*. 'In the end I ran because my training indicated that I was in good shape and I was getting fed up with all the fuss it was causing. So I went out and did the patriotic thing. But maybe next time I won't be so ready to do it. I'm not so young and fickle.'

Ovett channelled his efforts toward the Montreal Olympics as soon as he returned from Nice, but once again, he also had to sort out his future away from the running track. Having completed the first year of his college course he felt that his running had suffered, and he was faced with a choice between art and athletics.

With a glittering running career ahead of him the choice

may have seemed a simple one, but it was a serious dilemma to Steve. He sought the advice of his former art teacher at Varndean, Matt Bruce. 'I told Steve it was a decision he would have to make himself,' recalls Matt, now a professional artist. 'Art and running are two such individualistic areas that you have to give everything to one or the other. I pointed out to Steve that he could always come back to art, but he wouldn't be able to do that with his running. He went away, thought about it for a couple of days, and chose to stick with athletics.'

Depending on his parents for financial support, Ovett became a 'full time athlete' — a move both frowned upon and unprecedented in British athletics circles. His parents provided him with an ideal situation to prepare for the Olympic Games and, without the pressure of feeling obliged to sponsors or governing bodies, he had the freedom to guide his own future. And that future appeared to be the brightest one in the athletics world as the 1976 Olympics approached.

Three

A Breath of Fresh Air

1976 brought the culmination of another Olympiad. Four years of interval running, fartlek, weight training and general stretching of both mind and body ended in the ultimate test for hundreds of dedicated athletes throughout the world. It was no different for Steve Ovett — a little more tense, if anything. His winter work-outs had gone well and few people dared to argue against his achieving the two mammoth targets he set himself for 1976: to win the Olympic 800m and to break Fiasconaro's world record.

'He doesn't think that at the moment he is the greatest in the world or anything like that but he knows what he's got to do,' said Harry Wilson in *Athletics Weekly*. 'He's arrogant and self-confident, but not big-headed. He is still at the beginning of his career and by no means a polished athlete. I think he is the greatest talent we have ever had in Britain as a runner. He thinks, like myself, that training at international level is not a hit and miss affair. It requires careful planning. Steve is very single-minded and, above all, he is a good technician, which is very important. He can run the first lap of an 800m in 52 seconds and he's relaxed. That is the difference. When Steve runs, he is very relaxed and not struggling or straining.'

Most observers agreed with Wilson's assessment but reckoned that despite his immense strength for a twenty-year-old runner, Ovett needed a little more strength before he could confidently contemplate achieving his ambitions. And it was in the mud of the cross-country season where Steve sought that extra strength; although too much cross-country, with the Games so close at hand, might wreck his chances of success. Among his cross-country triumphs was an easy win in the South of Thames Championships on his home training patch of Stanmer Park, adjacent to Sussex University, on the outskirts of Brighton.

On 3rd January he won the Sussex senior cross-country title in controversial style at Bexhill. He had made a last minute switch from the Junior to the Senior event and the rule-book states that he wasn't, in fact, old enough to run in the senior race. Officials waived the rules, but Ovett's club-mate Peter Standing — who finished just behind him, in second place — lodged an official complaint and was so incensed about the circumstances that he left the Brighton club to join Windsor and Eton AC.

With some useful strengthening work behind him, Ovett flew out to oxygen-starved Lake Tahoe, 7,000 feet above sea-level in the California Pine Forests, at the beginning of April. Accompanied by Harry Wilson, he spent a month training at altitudes along with two of Britain's top distance runners — Tony Simmons and Ian Stewart. Although the trip cost his parents £800, it provided him with an invaluable launching pad for the season ahead.

The effects of such work appear in the long term and Ovett's opening races of the track season certainly didn't set the athletics world alight. He returned home in May, hoping to break David Jenkins' UK record in a 600m race at Crystal Palace, but the combined effects of jet lag and a strong wind resulted in a narrow win in the slow time of 78.5 — the final 100m taking 14.6.

Feeling he was lacking sharpness, Ovett ran some impressive 400m races and only some low-key 800m races. The philosophy behind his Olympic build-up was to avoid his major rivals and thus prevent them from knowing how to beat him in Montreal. After resisting a chance to face Mike Boit and Susanj at Gateshead, he said: 'I do want to race them, but only in the Olympics. That's when I'll be ready. The actual advantage I've got is that they don't know what sort of form I'm in.'

That approach was to cost him dearly, but all appeared to be going well when he won the selection trials in 1:46.7 — thus setting himself head and shoulders above his fellow Britons. Relaxed in the knowledged that he had qualified for Montreal in his main event, Ovett decided to tackle the 1500m trials. He found himself hopelessly boxed in for most of the race and even had to step on to the grass in-field at one stage. With just 70m left, however, he slipped between the two favourites, Frank Clement and Dave Moorcroft, then twisted his body round to wave at the crowd before winning in a time of 3:39.6.

Writing about 'this awesome display of talent' in *Athletics Weekly*, Mel Watman predicted that 'one of these days Ovett is going to produce a performance which will astound the world'. He produced it two weeks later in Helsinki, where he defeated world mile record holder John Walker over 800m. Covering the final lap in 50 seconds, it was a comfortable win over the Commonwealth Games 800m bronze medalist for Ovett. The New Zealander took the defeat to heart and ever since there has been especially keen rivalry and respect between the two men.

Such impressive form made Ovett an outsider in the medal stakes and local betting tumbled from 12–1 to 8–1. For the last two years he had made no secret of the fact that he had set his heart on Olympic success, but on the plane out of Canada he told Cliff Temple that he feared his lack of experience might let him down. Such fears proved to be prophetic.

With Mike Boit falling victim to the African boycott, the strong contenders for the dubious role of pre-Olympic 800m favourites were Rick Wohlhuter (the American who had fallen in the heats in Munich, but who was shaping up along similar lines to Dave Wottle, the reigning champion) and European Champion Luciano Susanj. The huge Cuban Alberto Juantorena was regarded as a 400m specialist and was therefore dismissed as a potential medal winner. But since finishing fourth behind Ovett in the 1973 European Junior Championships the tall Belgian Ivo Van

Damme had made huge strides — both literally and metaphorically — and was, like Ovett, rated as an outsider in the scramble for the bronze medal.

The renowned Irish half-miler 'Steve O'vett' (as his name was fed into the Olympic computer, and thus on to the scoreboard) had an easy passage in the third-round heat, coming first in 1:48.3 on the opening day of track competition in the Olympic Stadium. But the following day, Saturday, 24th July, brought a tough test for Ovett. He was drawn in the first semi-final, which contained a far better crop of two-lappers than the second semi-final, and had to finish in the first four to reach the Olympic 800m final.

In his first season of 800m running, Alberto Juantorena dominated the race from gun to tape. Pursued by Van Damme and India's Sriram Singh, Ovett was three metres ahead of the giant Cuban with 200m remaining. Juantorena and Van Damme sped past to fill first and second places (in 1:45.9 and 1:46.0 respectively). With the following day's final very much in mind, Ovett was content to use as little speed as possible over the final furlong and came home safely in third (1:46.1). Singh was the fourth qualifier for the final, with such notabley performers as James Robinson (USA) and Dr Thomas Wessinghage (West Germany) falling by the way side. The qualifiers in the slower semi-final were Rick Wohlhuter (USA), Carlo Grippo (Italy), Luciano Susanj (Yugoslavia) and Willi Wulbeck (West Germany).

To perform well in a nerve-racking Olympic final and make the thousands of training hours worthwhile, an athlete must not only feel that everything is running smoothly on the day but he must also avoid ill-luck. And fortune didn't favour Steve Ovett on Sunday, 25th July as he prepared for the supreme test of his youthful but dramatic career in the Olympic 800m final.

'I remember being worried because I had a pin missing from the number on my chest,' Ovett told Dave Cocksedge. 'I felt I'd better get something done about it straight away, but then I also remember telling myself: "God, you shouldn't be worried abut a pin missing from the top of your number on a day like this!" Anyway, I went up to the starter, got a pin, and made sure the number was secure. Then I thought, "well you're as ready as you'll ever be" and I went up to place on the stagger.

'I was choked about getting lane eight because I'm not experienced enough yet to run really well from right outside in a 300m stagger situation; and here I was getting stuffed in the most important race of all. I like to follow on the first lap; assess the pace, and plan my moves, but with this 300m in lanes business the guy in lane eight has no real chance. I just went off too slowly in the first 200m. That was where I blew the race. At the time, it was just the worst possible lane I could have had, and the way I ran proved it!'

Juantorena ripped down the back straight and was four yards up on everyone coming off the second bend. Going through half-way in 50.85, he was still full of running with Ovett ten yards down in fifth place. The unfavourable draw was a major factor in costing him the race, but his final undoing came when he used up his 'kick' attempting to stay in touch with the leader as they entered the second lap. Down the back straight (500m to 600m), Juantorena effectively collected the gold medal by maintaining his searing pace; only Wohlhuter and Van Damme made a desperate bid to catch him. Ovett was seventh coming off the final bend — his medal chances in tatters; but he managed to pass Susanj and Singh to clinch fifth place, two strides behind Willi Wulbeck, in a personal best of 1:45.44. Juantorena had breasted the tape in a new world and Olympic record of 1:43.5, with Van Damme collecting an unexpected silver medal and Wohlhuter came in third.

Even in retrospect, Ovett called it 'my least satisfying race'. And the Montreal scoreboard flashed confirmation of his disappointment:

1. Alberto Juantorena Cuba 1:43.50 (World Record)
2. Ivo Van Damme Belgium 1:43.86

3. Rick Wohlhuter	USA	1:44.12
4. Willi Wulbeck	West Germany	1:45.26
5. Steve Ovett	GB	1:45.44
6. Luciano Susanj	Yugoslavia	1:45.75
7. Sriram Singh	India	1:45.77
8. Carlo Grippo	Italy	1:48.39

Ovett's immediate post-race reaction was natural. The chance for glory had been in front of him and was gone. He was stunned by the suddenness of it all. 'My legs were dead after 300m, which was the first time I saw the other runners,' he said. 'I knew then that I couldn't catch them. The lane draw was a killer and I found it terribly difficult to gauge myself against men of this calibre. I only hope there'll be another time.'

What had seemed within his grasp at the start of the year had slipped away in the twinkling of an eye. Tactically, the race highlighted Ovett's inability to hold on to a fast first lap pace. It is, of course, easier to be wise after the event, but Ovett's almost paranoic wish to keep his form under wraps by not racing his major opponents prevented him from developing sufficient form to cope with an Olympic final. Later in his career his preparations for the Moscow Olympics seemed to prove that theory and show that he had learned from the experience of Montreal.

Nevertheless, a tired and disgruntled Ovett had the opportunity to put the disappointment of the 800m behind him when the heats of the 1500m started four days later. Steve won his heat in a personal best time of 3:37.9, the same as second-placed Thomas Wessinghage. After a slow early pace, when the runners almost trod on each other's toes for fear of taking the lead, the semi-final exploded into action. John Walker sped around the final turn, Canadian Dave Hill fell over, thus forcing Ovett to hurdle over him, and the rest were locked in a desperate battle to the tape.

As Walker charged towards victory in 3:39.65, Ovett and Coventry middle distance runner Dave Moorcroft were left in a contest of their own — which became more intense when Ovett glanced to his right and saw that it was his British team-mate who was challenging him. Moorcroft found the most strength as he dug deep into his reserves to finish third, while a lethargic-looking Ovett crossed the line in sixth place; his time of 3:40.34 lost him a place in the final by 0.4 second. 'I'm very tired after five hard races,' said Ovett, adding that he 'couldn't give a monkey's' about the 1500m. John Walker went on to win the final from Ivo Van Damme and Paul Wellman (West Germany) with Britain's Frank Clement fifth and Dave Moorcroft seventh.

In an exclusive *Sunday People* interview with David Barnes before the 1980 Olympics, Steve recalled that his experiences in Montreal made him disillusioned about the whole Olympic scene: 'I was into the spirit of international friendship and all that. I was carried away by the mystique but it didn't last long. When you get there, it hits you right in the face. You see people fighting for a gold to become a success in life. A gold medal and they're automatically swallowed up by PR firms.

'You're just another number, with your name tag and photograph. You're told when to feed. You're shoved into undignified dope tests at any time — usually when you can't oblige. A couple of team-mates come in drunk in the middle of the night when you are trying to get vital sleep. I suppose you can't blame them for enjoying themselves when they've been knocked out in the heats. But some performers know they have no chance before they even go to the Games!'

Ovett said that Britain sent a big team which meant lots of officials in blazers, heading for functions. 'They want everyone to see how many athletes they've brought to take part,' said Ovett. 'It means they really have to pack us into our accommodation. There were fifteen people in my apartment in Montreal. I was using the same toilet as four or five blokes. As an event, it just didn't meet my dreams.

'You can find a tube of Colmans mustard in your kit. Sportswear firms are shoving training stuff at you to wear. All you can see is signs for Pepsi and Coke. Guards walk round with guns. The public only sees a fraction ... when the gun goes. It took me a long time to get over the Games. I was dazed with the thoughts of failure — even though I did a personal best time. The athlete is almost doomed to failure. Only one person in four years out of the whole world's athletic population is right. Everyone else is wrong.'

Many people were prepared to dismiss Ovett's future hopes when he returned home. His career was at its lowest ebb since it swung into motion seven years earlier. But victories over John Walker, when retaining his AAA Championships title, and Mike Boit and Willi Wulbeck, at the IAC/Coca Cola meeting, helped to blunt his intense feelings of disappointment and sent him into his winter training with an air of hope for the future.

1976 had, in fact, brought a conclusion to the first chapter of Steve Ovett's running career. He had served his learning apprenticeship at international level and his personal nadir in Montreal was to be the springboard to his domination of the world middle distance scene. Harry Wilson had, for a long time, attempted to persuade Steve to concentrate on 1500m and miling, and the nightmare of the Olympic 800m final finally prompted the move. It was to be a significant watershed in his running career.

As Ovett built up his stamina on the winter cross country circuit once again, the British athletics scene in early 1977 was dominated by the emergence of Sebastian Coe. The Hallamshire Harrier's linear features and distinctive running style began to become familiar as he twice smashed the UK indoor 800m record and won the European Indoor 800m title in only a tenth of a second outside the world record.

Ovett, meanwhile, was building up quite a reputation in British cross-country circles. He handled seven and a half miles in mud with great ease in finishing a magnificent second place in the prestigious Inter Counties race, only 60m behind long distance expert David Black. In March, he competed in the senior national cross-country championships at Parliament Hills and came a creditable thirteenth.

It was all good grounding for the track season which lay ahead. A post-Olympic track season invariably gets under way with an air of anti-climax hanging over it. However, it often presents the ideal platform for those who, like Ovett, were deemed to have failed by the cruel measure of Olympic success, to restore their confidence and display their true capabilities. It was to be so for Steve Ovett.

As Britain celebrated the Queen's Silver Jubilee with miles of patriotic bunting and thousands of street parties, the athletics fraternity began to celebrate the dawning of the golden era of British athletics — heralded by the emergence of Steve Ovett as the world's number one miler.

In *Athletics Weekly*, Ovett assessed his chances of breaking onto the world miling scene on the eve of the start of the track season. 'I'm not very strong in terms of stamina yet,' he said. 'I need a few more years to build on my strength and stamina, then I think I'll be very good.' But as the season got underway, it became increasingly obvious that Ovett had found his true running niche.

Beneath the palm trees of Kingston, Jamaica, Ovett faced his first serious race of the year on 13th May. News of the race filtered back to Britain in the form of a typical early season result, tucked unobtrusively onto the foot of the sports pages. But the race was to prove one of the most significant Ovett ever contested. Not for the fact that he defeated Tanzania's world record holder Filbert Bayi over 1500m, but in this race the emerging American miler Steve Scott became the last man to defeat Ovett in a 1500m or mile race until August 1980. Both men clocked 3:39.8, with Ovett losing out on the photo-finish.

The following week Bayi gained revenge by defeating Ovett in a 3000m race during the Philips Night of Athletics Meeting at Crystal Palace. However, Ovett defeated Polish steeplechaser Bronislaw Malinowski and reduced his personal best by a full 25 seconds — a further indication that he was well on the way to a world class future at distances above 800 metres.

The Brighton man's physique appeared to have gained in strength over the autumn, winter and spring months and this was obviously a vital factor as he began to accumulate an impressive list of 1500m victories. Among them was the UK title, which he won at Cwmbran in a personal best time of 3:37.5. An impulsive wave to the crowd had cost him the British record by an agonising one-tenth of a second. It seemed inevitable that something special was on the proverbial cards and before the month was over he had set his first British record.

It came in front of a capacity 20,000 crowd at Crystal Palace when he challenged John Walker, Kenya's Wilson Waigwa and Ari Paunonen, the Finnish runner who had beaten Sebastian Coe in the previous year's European Junior Championship, in a classic mile confrontation. It was the perfect stage for Ovett to prove that British miling hadn't been dead and buried when Derek Ibbotson hung up his spikes in the fifties. After a reticent early pace Walker spurted clear with 250m remaining, but Ovett moved into overdrive in the home straight and stormed past the Olympic champion to set a new British record of 3:54.7.

It was a devastating display of talent by Ovett, who had accomplished his memorable victory with apparent ease. British athletics, which had been kept smouldering in the early seventies by Bedford and Foster, was in the process of being set alight. Athletics is, of course, not all about the few stars who steal the limelight, but the emergence of a world beater in Britain has a boosting effect at all levels of the sport and in 1977 Steve Ovett was doing exactly that.

He was not only making his mark on the middle distance scene. He was forming the reputation of being Britain's greatest ever runner. He drove his Range Rover up to Gateshead to run his second 5000m and played a leading role in one of the best twelve and a half lap track races ever held in Britain. Facing a strong field, headed by Ethiopia's amazing 34-year-old Miruts Yifter and including Dave

Black, Bernie Ford and Ian Stewart, he coped with the distance and ability field very comfortably. And he could have confidently expected to win any normal top class 5000m race with the 59 second last lap he produced to be placed eighth in the UK all-time list with a tremendous time of 13:25.0.

The race was, however, far from normal — it contained the diminutive, balding figure of Yifter, who was in the process of becoming one of the sport's legends. From 250m out, he rendered Ovett's feared 'kick' ineffective by opening a ten metre gap within the blink of an eye. Covering the final lap in 54.6 he finished 30m clear of Ovett at the tape. It was the first time the Ethiopian army corporal had raced in Britain and the impressive manner in which he shook off Ovett's challenge set him on the path to a glorious 5000m and 10,000m victory in the Moscow Olympics.

Ovett had his own plans for the Moscow Olympics. Returning to his task of dominating the world's top 1500m men at the Europa cup final in Helsinki, the pattern of his execution was becoming rather familiar. After a slow, bruising early pace ('We were so close together that we were breathing down each others' vests,' said Ovett), Ovett left Thomas Wessinghage, Ari Paunonen and Jurgen Straub for dead in the finishing straight, having been only sixth with 300m remaining.

Despite his slow winning time of 3:44.9 — half a second ahead of Wessinghage — Ovett's victory confirmed not just potential but his real talent in world terms. Following his 53 second last lap, Ovett declined to appear at the winners' press conference — thus further exacerbating his strained relations with sections of the Press. But Cliff Temple, writing in *The Sunday Times*, was as objective as ever: '... what the hell! The boy wins races, has a balanced approach to athletics (which can be a rarity in the international athlete) and, apart from being a tremendous talent, he's like a breath of fresh air to the sport.'

From being a breath of fresh air to the sport one week.

Steve Ovett moved towards becoming its biggest living legend the next. After missing his flight to Edinburgh, where he was due to run against John Walker in the Highland Games, Ovett surprised competitors and officials of the Dartford annual half-marathon by asking if he could compete, just half an hour before the start. Nobody objected, so Ovett went off with the leaders on the thirteen and a quarter mile race, run along lonely and twisting Kent lanes. He surprised the British class field of runners by sharing the pace with AAA Marathon champion Barry Watson before breaking clear with four miles remaining to win the longest race of his career by a margin of 21 second in a time of 65 minutes and 38 seconds — an astonishing achievement for a middle distance runner.

'I had just driven Matt up to the race and my legs were a little stiff when I got out of the car,' Ovett told Cliff Temple in *The Sunday Times*. 'So I asked the referee if I could run in the race too. I had meant to drop out after a few miles, but I felt good and carried on. Mind you, I could hardly walk for a couple of days afterwards.'

The race exemplified Ovett's impulsive approach to his running and further illustrated his unprecedented range of running capabilities. The latest twist in the career of the former English Schools' sprint champion baffled and amazed the athletics world. Said Ovett: 'I don't like to call myself a 1500m runner, or an 800m runner, or a 5000m runner. I just run because I enjoy it and because I enjoy winning. Sometimes athletes are too ready to put themselves into little boxes.'

With the supreme test of Ovett's adjustment of world miling and metric miling, in the World Cup, just fourteen days away, athletics coaches scratched their heads and opined that Ovett had gone too far this time. While being dubbed as the Muhammad Ali of the athletics world, Ovett said: 'Surely athletics is concerned with finding out about yourself, not repeating yourself, time and time again? I'm not trying to prove anything. I'm not attempting to be Britain's number one or the world's number one. I'm just being *me*.'

And Ovett just being himself caused further astonishment when the effects of the tough half-marathon seemed to enhance, rather than mar, his World Cup performance. John Walker and Thomas Wessinghage presented him with the strongest threat the athletics world could provide, and the two milers hoped to draw the sting out of his sprint finish, figuring that he would be vulnerable in a race which had a fast early pace. Wessinghage consequently led through the first lap in 56.4, with Walker going through 800m in 1:55.

The tall New Zealander still led at the bell, but Ovett moved menacingly on to his shoulder and characteristically struck 200m from home. Thrusting all of his power into a devastating burst around the final bend, he scattered the field and caused Walker to drop out of the race in a shattered stupor. Covering the last 100m in 11.8, Ovett waved at his parents on his way to cracking the UK record with a time of 3:34.6. Ovett had ended his storming season by proving that he was unquestionably the world's greatest middle distance runner in the best possible way, by destroying the Olympic champion. His impressive manner of execution led one sportswriter to comment, 'Steve Ovett is an astonishing animal and a young man born to run.'

The plaudits acclaiming his breakthrough into the world spotlight came thick, fast and deservedly. Invitations to every conceivable type of function poured through the letterbox of 8 Harrington Villas every morning — a great temptation to a man who had competed a hard year's work. But Ovett, who was also voted Athlete of the Year by the Athletics Writers' Association, was determined not to be swayed from his course. 'You have to be single-minded,' he said. 'If I accepted every invitation I'd never be at home and I like being at home.'

Writing in *The Times*, Cliff Temple emphasised a growing feeling about the home loving king of the track and pinpointed Ovett's uniqueness when he wrote: 'Optimism about Ovett's career is not misplaced. Athletics is a sport littered with memories of those who had tremendous talent as youngsters but who either could not cope with the increasing pressure of training or who lacked sufficient motivation. Their places are taken by those with limited talent but with a burning desire to overcome those limitations. Ovett is a young man who has always been an outstanding runner who has adjusted to higher planes, both mentally and physically.'

Steve Ovett had adjusted to the world middle distance scene and had overcome the bitter disappointment of Olympic failure. At the age of twenty-one he had developed into the greatest running talent the world had ever seen.

Four

Another Competitor

Steve Ovett's concentration on 1500 metre and mile racing in the Silver Jubilee Year of 1978 took him to the very pinnacle of world athletics, but also allowed another potential world beater to emerge and give his career an unexpected twist. That twist appeared in the shape of twenty-year-old Loughborough University student Sebastian Coe. For four years, Ovett had been one of Britain's most precocious and promising athletic talents as he forged his way to the top — with older, seasoned runners to aim at all of the way. Suddenly, Coe's shadow appeared on the horizon as a real threat to his claim as Britain's number one 800m runner.

At the Coca Cola meeting, Coe had finished a mere two-tenths of a second behind Mike Boit to break Andy Carter's UK 800m record in a startling time of 1:45.0. The record had always eluded Ovett, whose best time was nearly half a second slower. Coe's spectacular arrival on the international scene must have given Ovett a great deal to think about during the long winter months, as he prepared for the major championship of 1978.

Although Ovett's superior strength and experience must have made him confident of dealing with Coe's threat, he had almost completely ignored the 800m in 1977 and had to decide whether he still had a future in the two-lap event. Coe added fuel to the flames of rivalry beginning to kindle when he remarked in an *Athletics Weekly* interview with Jon Wigley: 'The thought of racing Ovett over 800m doesn't get me worked up. He is another competitor, albeit a very good one ... the world is full of good competitors.'

Behind the frail looking facade was a young man with an attitude as strikingly determined as the one which took Steve Ovett to the top. A much awaited confrontation was to come later in the year, but Ovett was enjoying his running as much as ever and once again he prepared for another tough year by turning to the cross country season.

In December he came sixth in the IAC event at Crystal Palace, behind such notable distance runners as Yifter and his fellow Ethiopian Eshetu Tura and then he collected three prestigious titles early in the New Year. After winning the Sussex championships for the third successive year, Steve represented England in the Northern Banks International in Belfast and won by twelve seconds from Scotland's Nat Muir. Snow, mud and ice could not prevent him from romping to victory in the coveted Inter Counties Championships at Derby; he covered the seven and a half mile course in 37:40 — eleven seconds ahead of Welsh distance running star Steve Jones.

Such was the reputation Ovett was building on the cross-country circuit that he was the clear favourite to win the 1978 National at Leeds in March. Steve had been forced to cope with the pressure of being favourite in almost every race since he picked up a pair of running spikes and the disastrous start he made must have had some roots in the pressure put upon him. It could be argued that Ovett's desire to push himself to the limits the previous week, when he stepped up his weekly training mileage from 100 to 168 : 'just to see how it felt', was another example of his tremendous talent. Nevertheless, Ovett had to work hard to get in touch with the leaders, and only managed to pull back several places in the closing stages to clinch fourth place.

Being judged to have: 'failed' with such a performance was a true indication of Ovett's standing in the athletics world. Another was his refusal to run for England in the World Cross Country Championships at Glasgow — a chance which his performance at Leeds had earned him. Moreover, he wrote to the AAA informing them of his decision not to run in the summer's Commonwealth Games in Canada as he intended to concentrate his efforts on the more prestigious European Championships. Another major factor which influenced his decision was his parents' inability to make the trip to Edmonton to cheer him on.

Whatever the reason, Ovett had the satisfaction of being in the position where he could make his own decisions, in contrast to four years earlier when he had unluckily missed out on selection. The eighteen-year-old who had been so intensely geared towards success in Rome and the twenty-year-old who was desperate for Olympic glory had changed; perhaps 'matured' is a more appropriate adjective. In an interview with Patrick Collins in the London *Evening News*, he claimed that he didn't have any 'specific goals'. Involvement with handicapped children had helped him to put his athletics in perspective and, following his experience in Montreal, Ovett said he had realised 'how stupid it is to think that an Olympic Gold medal could be the answer to everything. It's just one race on one day,' he said. 'I could miss out on Moscow altogether and it wouldn't be the end of my world.'

However, Ovett's athletic aim was undoubtedly to strike gold in the Moscow Olympics and the 1978 track season would be a vital stage in his preparations. His first major race could not have provided a stiffer test: a 3000m confrontation with Kenya's Henry Rono, fresh from setting world records at 10,000 and 5000m, in the Philips Night of Athletics meeting at Crystal Palace. Despite suffering from a septic tooth, Ovett finished five seconds behind Rono (in 7:48.4). On the same track, at the beginning of June, he smashed Brendan Foster's UK 2000m record by recording the fastest time ever run — 4:57.8. The following week he defeated East Germany's Jurgen Straub, a man for whom he holds a great deal of respect, over 1500m in the UK/GDR match at Crystal Palace.

Ovett embarked on a mini European tour as part of his preparation for the European Championships in Prague.

He easily defeated Steve Scott over 1500m in 3:37.6 in the Swedish city of Malmo, and repeated his victory over the American in Dublin (3:55.7 for the mile) and Oslo (3:35.8 for the metric mile). The victories helped to increase Ovett's reputation as the world's number one middle-distance runner, but an 800m run of 1:45.4 in Turku, Finland, which equalled his personal best, persuaded him that he still had a future in the two lap race and he consequently put his name down to run both races in Prague.

Such formidable form prompted the following comments from Rod Dixon, the Olympic 5000m bronze medalist: 'Steve is capable of running under 3 minutes 50 seconds for the mile during his build-up to Moscow, and also of grabbing a world record for the 1500m. For my money he's the Juantorena of the 1500m and I would not like to back anybody to beat him. Over the next two years his form could be one of the most exciting things in world class athletics.'

The New Zealander was to be proved unmistakably accurate but in the build-up to Prague suddenly Ovett had competition — and from fellow Britons. At the Ivo Van Damme Memorial meeting in Brussels Sebastian Coe smashed his UK 800m record with an incredible time of 1:44.3 which was over a second faster than Ovett had ever clocked. Then Dave Moorcroft forced his way into the metric mile reckonings by defeating Filbert Bayi in the world-class time of 3:34.48 to take the Commonwealth Games title in Canada.

The stage was set for some stirring races in the Czech capital, but before Ovett flew out to Prague he won a mile race in the Rotary Watches International in 3:57.7 at Crystal Palace. Once again, he gesticulated wildly to the crowd in the home straight and once again the Press latched onto him as a denigrator of his fellow competitors, arrogant, brash Ovett ... and such a contrast to the charming young Coe.

Ovett had been Britain's premier 800m runner from 1974

until Coe's emergence in 1977, yet Coe topped the world rankings in 1978. A foot race between these two Britons was now eagerly awaited like no other in history. So far no promoter had managed to match them but the lure of major championship gold was now too great to keep the sleek front runner from Sheffield and the devastating 'kicker' from Brighton apart. They comprised constrasting public images, contrasting styles, contrasting figures and contrasting personalities. All was set for a mighty showdown.

After his Brussels run, Coe was confident he could run the sting out of Ovett's finish, and Ovett, in turn, was sure that he could stay with Coe's pace and then 'take' him in the home straight. The two Englishmen sailed through the heats and semi-finals in the Rosicky Stadium, Coe won his semi in 1:47.4, ahead of the East German Andreas Busse, while Ovett also won from an East German, Olaf Beyer in 1:46.5.

The scene was set for the British showdown in the final; the feeling that it was to be a two horse race having been reinforced when third favourite Willi Wulbeck failed to turn up for his heat. As expected, Coe blasted away but nobody had anticipated the almost suicidal pace at which he set off. Clocking 49.3 for the first lap, Coe failed to shake off Beyer, Ovett and Busse, who were all within striking distance at the bell. Coe held on to his lead down the back straight (500–600m) as Ovett gathered for the 'kill', a stride behind.

Entering the final straight, Coe was just half a stride up on Ovett, with Beyer's shadow looming ominously behind them. Ovett sailed past Coe with 70m left and, with the Loughborough student fading badly, he must have been mentally clearing a place on his sideboard for the gold medal. But the East German Beyer was thinking along the same lines and his muscular, blue-vested figure stormed past to snatch victory in 1:43.8 — two seconds faster than his previous best time at the distance. Ovett clipped 0.2 seconds from Coe's UK record with a time of 1:44.1 in second place, while Coe's break neck early pace was sufficient to earn him a bronze medal in 1:44.8.

Coe and Ovett had given everything. But the East German found himself in the perfect position coming off the last bend and had sufficient energy to do what many had failed to do in the past two years; to outkick Ovett in the home straight. The race was one of the most exhilarating in a recent major championship. And Ovett was far from disappointed at having gained his second European Championship silver medal, when he was capable of taking the gold on both occasions. He told Mel Watman in *Athletics Weekly*: 'Considering that I never trained for the 800m, and I only raced three times in almost over two years over 800m, to get the silver medal with that sort of background and to break the UK record was really pleasing. The 800m was just something to keep me off the training track really. I waited on Seb round the final bend and I worked hard from 200m out. Seb did everything he could, I did everything I could — we were just beaten by a better man on the day. I mean being beaten by a man that runs 1 minute 43.8 seconds is no disgrace ... as far as I'm concerned it was a success. I could not have wished for more.'

Beyer's achievement even amazed the East Germans. The 21-year-old Potsdam University student, who was on military service at the time, said, 'I made up my mind before the start to fight for victory, but I would have been happy with any medal. When I drew level with the two British runners in the finishing straight and felt quite strong, I started to feel I could beat Ovett.' Suspicions were rife as to how Beyer had managed to raise his performance to such a high degree. In his autobiography *Running Free*, Sebastion Coe wrote: 'The extraordinary thing about Beyer was that Steve and I didn't see him again for ages. As he ran through the finishing line he was wrapped in blankets by two officials and hurried from the arena, instead of going off on a lap of honour, as you would expect from someone who had just won a European title. Geoff

Capes and David Jenkins say that he walked off with his eyes completely slack. And he then went missing. We were informed that he had provided his urine sample within thirteen minutes of running 1 minute 43 seconds, which is unusual to say the least. It took Steve and me almost an hour and a half and we only saw Beyer again at the victory ceremony.'

Ovett thought Beyer's win was due to more conventional means: 'I think with Beyer, it was just one of those races where you're going to get that sort of improvement,' he told Mel Watman. 'Everybody was running hard from the word go. We had two pacemakers really with Seb and myself and he just took it up over the last 60 or 70 yards. Two men fight each other and you get picked off at the finish. Outsiders come through in races when no pressure is on them, and I think that was probably the case with Beyer. We were taking all the pressure, we were expected to come one and two in no matter what order; all he had to do was cling on to us and that is exactly what he did and it paid dividends. It was our mistake and his benefit.'

So with two European silver medals, Ovett desperately wanted to win the gold in the 1500m. Having once again come through the qualifying rounds with no problems, he went into the final as favourite, but many people believed the 800m defeat would adversely affect his attitude. But, said Harry Wilson in *Athletics Weekly*, 'It made him even more certain that he was unbeatable in the 1500m. I could not believe that the media had any doubts about him. They were naming Moorcroft as the favourite, Loikkanen as a danger. All thinking men after the 800m would have said that with Ovett running the fastest 800m in his life there was nobody going to beat him. That was Steve's attitude. And he was right.'

Beyer also reached the final and he made the early pace, with Jurgen Straub leading at the bell. Anti Loikkanen (Finland) kicked down the back straight but he and the rest of the field were powerless to respond to Ovett's traditional spurt 200m from home. A 10m gap immediately opened as the field desperately struggled to make up the lost ground. Ovett floated to victory in the home straight in 3:35.6. He showed no signs of losing as he had done in the 800m and even turned to face his pursuers 80m out and gave them a cheeky two handed wave, a broad grin spread across his face. Irish runner Eamonn Coghlan pipped Dave Moorcroft for silver, a second behind Ovett. The quality of Ovett's victory was underlined by some of the non-medalists: Wessinghage (fourth), Straub (seventh). Beyer (ninth) and Plachy (twelfth).

Thus Ovett convincingly gained his first major championship gold medal and continued Britains's fine tradition in the European 1500m, established by Sydney Wooderson (1938), Roger Bannister (1954), Brian Hewson (1958) and John Whetton (1969). He also became only the second British athlete, behind Alan Pascoe, to win three European medals in individual events. He was, however, the only winner who wouldn't speak either to the official Czech 'track-side quotes' man or appear at the traditional post presentation conference.

Instead, Ovett made for his parents' hotel where, after being unable to get anything to eat, he sat sipping orange juice and spoke to Cliff Temple of *The Sunday Times*. A hollow-eyed and tired figure after his five tough races in six days, he admitted, 'I haven't really enjoyed these championships and I'll be glad to get back to Brighton. In fact I wanted to get home on the first day out here. I don't really know what I feel. There's no great urge to get drunk in celebration or anything like that. I suppose I just feel sort of numb and relieved that it's all over. There's been a lot of tension before the races, particularly the 800m. As for the 1500m, I knew I was fit, strong and fast, but there's always the chance that something will happen: you'll get pushed or bumped out the wrong moment, and then you can't re-run it. Not for another four years anyway. My burst over the final 200m is not my only tactic, but it's my best.

'They knew I was going to go from the 200 mark, and I moved out with 200 to go, almost said that I'm going to go now, and I beat all of them quite convincingly. It was very pleasing because I said to them try and beat me. I didn't try to surprise them with different tactics or anything like that. I know it sounds rather blasé but it's the way that I set about it.'

As Britain's only gold medalist, Steve faced a gaggle of reporters and TV cameras at Gatwick Airport. He pushed past them and jumped on the first train to Brighton. That evening he was in his favourite local drinking Harvey's Real Ale with his old college friends. After his Prague efforts, Ovett felt 'shattered' and the only training he did was confined to jogging. Nevertheless he gained a classic victory in the IAC/Coca Cola meeting at Crystal Palace when he finished ahead of Henry Rono in a world outdoor best of 8:13.5.

It was a thrilling race. The bunched field passed the mile mark in 4:08.8 and Rono tried to break clear with a 61 second sixth lap. But Ovett stuck with him and kicked off the final bend, waving as he passed Rono. Such an impressive victory over Kenya's double world record holder and Commonwealth Games champion helped to make up for the disappointment of losing his UK 800m record to Coe half an hour earlier: the Sheffield runner knocked a tenth of a second off Ovett's record with his time of 1:44.0. And a few weeks later, Ovett received a further boost when Rono was asked if he looked upon himself as the best runner in the world, 'No,' he replied in broken English, 'this guy Steve Ovett, you know, Steve Ovett is a tough guy.'

Ovett's trail-blazing season wasn't over yet. With plenty of good running left in his legs and no real opposition to aim at, he turned to the clock for the first time since his early career. As he told Mel Watman: 'I ran out of opposition and the only thing I had to go for was a good time. It was just a last resort and I don't think I've got the appetite for world records. I don't think I ever will have. It seems pointless to me.'

Within a year, Ovett's opinions were turned on their

head. But he jetted out to Oslo with the intention of 'stretching out and chasing the world record'. In arctic conditions, the local pacemaker couldn't maintain the pace and dropped out when Ovett shouted at him to 'go faster'. Nevertheless, the halfway time of 1:55.2 was still on schedule to better the European record (3:52.5). The cold, rain-drenched track and lack of opposition proved too much, but Ovett hacked 1.4 seconds off the British record in clocking 3:52.8 — the eighth fastest mile of all time.

Steve ended the 1978 season in style by running the Golden Mile in front of a 60,000 crowd in Tokyo's Olympic Stadium on 25th September. He had hoped to chase John Walker's world record (3:49.4) but after a complicated arrival in the Japanese capital he found it difficult to acclimatise to the conditions and ended up being satisfied with another victory. His familiar 'wait and kick' tactics took him past Rod Dixon with 300m left and saw him defeat Wessinghage and Scott in relaxed style. Although Ovett's row with the Press continued throughout the winter, he couldn't have been more popular with the British sports public. When he received the *Daily Express* Sportsman of the Year Award, he revealed more of the human side of his character by bursting into tears. 'It's been a lovely day,' he said, 'I was very moved when I saw myself at the medal ceremony in Prague. You work very hard, and you don't always get the emotion of it all. Well you get plenty of emotion on a day like today.'

Ovett was sitting on top of the athletics world after his exploits in the 1977 and 1978 track seasons. And former Olympic steeplechase bronze medalist John Disley underlined the feeling in the athletics world when he remarked in *Athletics Weekly*, 'I think Ovett is the finest runner I have ever seen. I think he is the greatest runner that Britain has ever produced in terms of natural talent and range of ability. It is that feeling of animal power Ovett has got.'

1979 was to have been a 'quiet' year for Steve Ovett. He and Harry Wilson wanted it that way in preparation for the following year's Olympic Games. But two important factors conspired to alter those plans.

After finishing sixth (behind winner Mike McLeod) in the National Cross-Country championships, Ovett easily won his first race of the track season by defeating Wessinghage over 1500m in a match between UK, West Germany, Poland and Switzerland in Bremen on 3rd June. The following day he pushed himself a little harder to win a 1500m race in Nijmegen, Holland in 3:37.9. It seemed like a conventional start to a track season, but it had far-reaching consequences.

Ovett's Nijmegen race angered British Amateur Athletic Board Officials, who claimed they had not given him permission to compete. But the Brighton man insisted that the meeting organiser Jos Hermens had obtained a permit on his behalf. Steve's decision not to run for Britain in the European Cup had exacerbated the situation and he was drawn into a confrontation with Britain's top athletics administrators which was to bring to light the enormous gulf that exists between them and the top athletes.

The British Board was pitched into total confusion about Ovett's Dutch race. General Secretary David Shaw, who had been appointed in an attempt to close the rift between athletes and officials, said, 'So far as we are concerned it is becoming apparent that no permission was granted.' A BAAB Committee enquiry ensued, following which a decision was made to take no action against Ovett. They concluded that a series of 'misunderstandings' led to the confused situation; an indictment of their own administration and management.

The decision angered officials, press and athletes returning home from the European Cup semi-finals in Malmo, Sweden. One newspaper commented: 'Most athletes do not have to be treated like schoolchildren but the Board seem frightened of Ovett's genius. He is an individual who likes to do things his own way, but he appears to have breached the normal standards of behaviour on this occasion and the Board have condoned it.'

The whole argument about whether athletes should be allowed to prepare in their own way for Olympic competition without being pressurised into running for their country was also brought into focus once again. Two years earlier Ovett had laid down his attitude in *Athletics Weekly*: 'I run to please myself,' he said. 'I'm not here to serve other people. That's always been my policy towards my athletics. I'll do my bargaining and bartering with the Board, but they've got to appreciate that I'm an amateur and I run as I please mainly ... so I'll select my races and run the ones I feel are best for me, and if that causes an uproar, then I'm sorry. But I'll still do it.'

Confusion turned to turmoil as Ovett became the subject in an argument between the AAA and BAAB about which governing body should have the ultimate say in deciding whether athletes could run abroad or not. The AAA had not been informed that the BAAB had given Ovett permission to run in the Golden Mile in Oslo. In retaliation, the AAA refused Ovett permission to run in a race in Dublin unless he guaranteed to take part in their championships, which he had intended to do anyway. Upset by their attitude, Ovett pulled out of the AAA championships and was forced to inform the BAAB that he would be unable to defend his Golden Mile title because he felt he needed the Dublin race to 'sharpen up' for the Golden Mile.

Confused? Surely! But not as much as Britain's athletics fraternity who have been forced to toe the line with a multiplicity of governing bodies. Events, nevertheless, took a dramatic turn on the evening prior to the Dublin meeting. The AAA decided to reverse their decision and grant him permission to run, although they received no guarantees that he would compete in their championships. Steve Ovett had struck a significant blow in the battle for the athlete's freedom.

Officials of the BAAB and AAA announced that they had changed their minds because they wanted to help Ovett 'achieve his objectives in athletics', which was a remarkable change in attitude from some of the men who had made such a great issue about his Nijmegen row. Inevitably, Ovett came in for criticism. One official claimed that he was 'acting like a big spoiled kid' and England team Manager Doug Goodman remarked, 'There are some athletes you have to treat like silk and Ovett is one of them'.

The media also joined in the portrayal of Ovett as a selfish rebel. They argued that Ovett enjoyed 'taking on the establishment'. But the issues at stake were more fundamental: should an amateur sportsman be subjected to a restriction of freedom which makes a mockery of the very 'amateur' image of athletics that many professional officials endeavour to uphold? Ovett was fighting for the right to prepare for the 1980 Olympics in the manner he felt would give him the best chance of succeeding.

Arriving at Dublin, Ovett was in no mood for enjoying his moral victory. 'I've had a lot of mental strain in the last two weeks and wasted a lot of energy and that's no way to prepare for a series of tough races,' he told reporters. 'If I had not got permission at the eleventh hour for this event it would have meant three weeks out of competitive racing for me at the height of the season.'

He consequently lacked his usual 'sparkle' on the track, but defeated Jozef Plachy over 800m in 1:46.17. In a rare post-race press conference, he told reporters that 1979 was now a 'dead year' for him, because of external pressures. Indeed the late *Daily Telegraph* athletics correspondent James Coote wrote, 'Although he expressed a lack of concern over what is written or said, his face and general demeanour bore marks of tension not usually there, proving that the last few weeks have, whatever he says, affected him greatly.'

The other major factor which altered Ovett's plans for a quiet season and which helped to divert the spotlight from his running was beginning to emerge. In Oslo, Sebastian Coe had stunned the athletics world by smashing Alberto Juantorena's world 800m record of 1:43.44 with an astonishing time of 1:42.33 — more than two seconds faster than Ovett's best two-lap time. After the race Coe said that he was aiming mainly for the 1500m at the Moscow Olympics and felt that the metric mile would be his best distance.

Ovett's controversial start to the season, meanwhile, continued to smoulder. He finally decided to compete in the AAA championships 1500m and won the title comfortably in 3:39.1. But the victory was overshadowed by his conduct in the heats when he ran the last 30m diagonally across the track to end up crossing the line in lane eight. One journalist summed up the media's feeling that Ovett's actions unnecessarily denigrated his fellow competitors by alleging that such behaviour 'indicates a high degree of conceit and arrogance. To treat one's fellow participants with such contempt is an act which, in itself, is beyond contempt.'

Darlington's promising young runner Paul Harker, who finished behind Ovett in that race, gave me his views of the incident: 'Coming off the final bend, Steve sprinted away and onto the long-jump run-way, then back on to the track again. I thought it was okay, that sort of thing doesn't bother me in the slightest. It's just a show piece for the crowd. If I was as good as Steve I would probably do the same thing.

'A lot of people failed to mention what Ovett did after the race. He dashed straight across to the disabled pen and spent half an hour talking to the wheelchair bound spectators and signing autographs. He's a great bloke and mixes well with the other runners.' Such a view of Ovett's home straight antics and their effect on his fellow competitors are, of course, dependent upon the individual and one of his rivals has said his over-riding ambition is to see Ovett fall flat on his face after delivering a premature victory salute.

Before the final, Ovett had endeavoured to clear the air of his controversial season in a BBC TV interview with David Coleman. 'I think it's only been my sheer bloody-mindedness that's carried me through the past three weeks of arguing and bad organisation of the governing body,' he fumed. 'Anyone else of, shall we say, lesser character, would have succumbed to the pressure put upon them a long time ago. In those three weeks I've done more political arguing than training, and that can't be good for any athlete.'

Accused of competing abroad more often than in domestic races, Ovett commented: 'That just doesn't stand up to analysis. I've competed for my club more often than for anybody else. And I'm not competing in the Golden Mile in Oslo; so their accusations just don't hold up when you examine the facts. I made my plans clear at the start of 1979: that I was low-keying the whole season. No big races. But the British Press can't accept that I'm bypassing big races and once again I'm accused of being unpatriotic. But the BAAB must understand that I feel I've earned a break.

'I've run in four Europa Cup races and won all four, I've won the World Cup 1500m and the Golden Mile in Tokyo last year. Now I want a break. They *must* realise that I've done my bit and they must allow me to choose my own way of preparing for Moscow. But they have said "No, you must compete here and there and there, and if you don't we will stop you competing in the races you want to do for your Olympic preparation." I don't like to have a loaded gun held up to my head, and I will therefore be as bloody-minded as they are.'

Ovett said that he wanted to train in his own way for Moscow in Britain. 'I don't need to go and train in the sun for three months or anything like that. I have my own routine here, and that's the best way for me. I'm not asking for anything except to be left alone to prepare in my own way. Maybe I'm wrong, but at least that's all on my own organisation. If I'm wrong and this is not the best way to prepare, I've only myself to blame. Let us get on with it, and we'll be there in Moscow — but what I don't want is all these stupid barriers put in my way. If people thing I'm an arrogant bastard for doing things my own way, then that's what I am. But I'll still do it. But I am patriotic in my own way. Press my doorbell and it rings "Rule Britannia". That's the truth'.

On the subject of the Golden Mile, he concluded: 'The race has got to be held here in Britain. We are supplying four milers out of a field of twelve for the race, and if we have that many in it, we should hold it here in front of the British public and not have to trek over to Oslo for it. I've beaten the world's best in Dusseldorf and everyone who turned up in Tokyo, and now if the best milers in the world want to take me on, they must come here to do it. I'll race anyone on my home ground in front of my own crowd. I've proved I'm the best and I'm sick of chasing races around the world. If they want to beat me they must come here and race me — that's the right of the world champion, surely?'

A possible Ovett/Coe clash in the Golden Mile was averted because of the authorities. And Ovett was bitter. 'The authorities should believe me when I tell them when and where I need to race,' he said. 'I know I'm the best in the world, it will be a hollow victory for whoever wins the race.'

Officials, press and anti-Ovett members of the athletics fraternity were therefore all the more delighted when Sebastian Coe — with a previous best mile time of 3:57.7 — chopped 0.4 seconds off the world record in the Golden Mile. He left the world's top milers – Steve Scott, Craig Masback, Eamonn Coghlan, John Robson, John Walker, Graham Williamson, Thomas Wessinghage and Dave Moorcroft – for dead as he floated to a new record of 3:49.0. It was an astonishing achievement and one which seriously threatened Ovett's claims to be the world's number one miler. Following the race Coe said, 'I do not feel, in any way, that I have achieved a hollow victory.'

It certainly was not. And Ovett had the humility to recognise it. After watching the race at home on TV with his parents he said, 'Congratulations to Seb, he is running brilliantly at the moment. To be honest, when you hear times like that they can be quite frightening.' Ovett concluded by setting himself up for embarrassment at the end of the season when he added, 'It doesn't change anything. I don't get caught up in times. I never run against the clock. I run against men on the day.'

The events surrounding Coe's third world record in 41 days in Zurich on 15th August, however, conspired to alter the whole emphasis of Ovett's racing philosophy. Ovett wanted to face Coe in the 1500m to settle the speculation about which runner was truly the world's greatest middle distance runner. Ovett's AAA official friend Andy Norman insisted that Ovett had been accepted, but meeting director Res Bruegger was not interested in staging the race the whole world wanted to see.

Herr Bruegger was more concerned about Coe's record attempt and banned Ovett from the 1500m saying, 'The crowd don't want a repeat of the cat and mouse affair in last year's European Championships.' Thus, as Coe set a new record of 3:32.03, Ovett was winning an insignificant 600m race at Crystal Palace. His chances of forcing a confrontation were dampened by Coe's post-race comments. 'Don't let the prospect of our beating each other become an obsession,' he pleaded. 'It's crazy to concentrate on one opponent.'

Coe denied avoiding Ovett, adding: 'From the age of ten I've never geared my training to suit other individuals. My race schedule this year was made in January and my objective was the 800m world record in August, but it all happened sooner than I expected. If I had failed to break the 1500m record in Zurich I would have run against Steve over 1500m in Brussels on 4th September.' Ovett, however, maintained two years later that the reason he didn't face Coe in Zurich was at the Sheffield man's insistence. 'He wouldn't face me in the race,' claimed Ovett.

But Coe wasn't the only thing on Ovett's mind in August

1979. On 17th August he defeated Craig Masback over the mile in 3:54.9 in West Berlin, ran a 4 × 800m relay leg at Crystal Palace the next day and 24 hours later was pipped into second place by America's James Robinson over 800m in Cologne, clocking his fastest time of the season (1:45.0). The hectic schedule was not another example of Ovett's impetuosity. As he explained, 'I've never had three races in three days before. The idea was to simulate the tough Olympic conditions'.

After an eight day rest, Ovett shattered his 'quiet' season. The man who wasn't interested in chasing records lost a great deal of the mystique he had built around himself by chasing Coe's records. Good pacemaking by Pete Browne and Thomas Wessinghage presented Ovett with the ideal opportunity to prove that world records were within his grasp, too, in the Rotary Watches Meeting at Crystal Palace. Only on the final lap of the mile did Ovett fall behind Coe's world record pace. Had he kicked at the bell, as Coe had done in Olso, the record would have been his. Nevertheless, his kick with 250m left helped to clock the third fastest mile ever — 3:49.57. Ovett became the third man, behind Walker and Coe, to crack 3:50 for the mile. His time was a UK all-comers record, the fastest mile time recorded on a British track, and his 1500m time of 3:34.0 was also a personal best. Ovett had spoken his message loud and clear. Watching from the Main Stand, Coe said, 'It was as perfect a race as I've ever seen ... a real classy win.' It was becoming increasingly likely that the two men wouldn't meet before the Olympics, but Thomas Wessinghage — who recorded the fourth fastest ever mile time, in second place — said, 'Ovett would beat Coe. I don't think Coe has the answer to Ovett's exceptional finishing kick.'

Robbed of the chance to measure against Coe in person, Ovett was attacking his times. His quiet season and disdain for records and times were unashamedly cast aside. Ovett explained the seemingly hypocritical stance he was adopting to David Barnes in the *Sunday People*: 'I wasn't jealous, but I set my target because suddenly I was being described as a one-paced runner with Seb the undisputed number one. I was a bit upset that, year after year, I ran well only to have it all washed aside.'

Four days later, he attacked Coe's 1500m record in front of 45,000 Belgians at The Ivo Van Damme Memorial Meeting in Brussels. Ovett passed half-way in 1:53.0—one fifth of a second inside record schedule—but he fell behind schedule when Willi Wulbeck took over the pacemaking on the penultimate lap. Ovett once again held back fractionally too long and narrowly missed the record after a devastating final 300m. His time of 3:32.11 was a mere one-hundredth of a second (or three inches) away from equalling Coe's record.

'I was obviously disappointed in missing the record by such a narrow margin,' he said afterwards. 'But I was encouraged that I could produce two such fast performances within a space of four days. No one else has achieved this and it has given me a tremendous confidence boost for the Moscow Olympics. World records are made to be beaten. On the other hand, an important victory, an Olympic title—that's what interests me. The battle of man against man is the only thing which counts, in my opinion. People say I don't go it alone early enough in my record attempts but the truth is I'm fighting against myself. I only get worked up when there's someone in front of me. I tend to lose interest when I can't be caught.'

Ovett ended his unusual season with two further confidence boosting mile wins, which took his unbeaten 1500m/mile record to almost three complete seasons. He clocked 3:56.6 in winning his first Emsley Carr Mile title, ahead of Omer Khalifa and Mike McLeod, at Gateshead and then recorded 3:55.3 in winning the Coca Cola Mile at Crystal Palace in September. Ovett and Coe were named in the inaugural BAAB elite squad, which guarantees Britain's top seven athletes exemption from the Olympic trials. The idea paid dividends when four of the seven collected gold medals in Moscow.

Steve flew out to Trinidad in September for a well earned holiday with his girlfriend Rachel Waller, a nineteen-year-old model from Kent, whom he had met earlier in the year. Behind him was a season in which he had come to terms with two factors which threatened to eclipse him: opposition from the authorities and Coe's domination of the middle distance running scene. Ahead of him, everything was set for a classic Olympic confrontation in 1980.

Five

Any Idiot Can Become an Olympic Champion

1980 was arguably the most successful year British athletics has ever enjoyed and it was dominated by talk of the race everybody wanted to see: Ovett versus Coe. In pubs and clubs from John O'Groats to Lands End there were a hundred theories about who would win, how they would win, and by how much. The athletics writers and figures from the athletics world added their opinions and one national newspaper even consulted a computer to predict the outcome.

The sports columns were swamped with stories about the noble nice guy from Sheffield and the brash, balding runner from Brighton. Speculation about the possible British boycott, requested by the Government following Russia's invasion of Afghanistan, and the boycott by such Western nations as West Germany and the USA took a back seat in the build-up of the 'sporting clash of the century'.

As far removed from the raging publicity as possible, Coe trained in the Italian hills until May, crowning his visit with a resounding victory in the 'Golden Shoe' road race near Milan. Ovett, meanwhile, was reaping the rewards from his Press battles. No reporters thought of bothering him, with little chance of obtaining quotes. He proved that his winter work had gone to plan by returning a staggering time of 14 minutes and 52 seconds for a 3 mile 500 yard stage in the Southern Road Relay Championships. Starting 89 seconds from the leader in seventh place, Ovett showed no fatigue in ending his leg with an 18 second lead for Brighton.

Ovett then began his globe-trotting preparations for Moscow by defeating Steve Scott in a 3000m race in Houston, USA, and Filbert Bayi in a 1500m race in Jamaica. It was a promising opening to the season but his efforts to keep a low pre-Olympic profile soon fell to pieces.

Deprived of a tilt at an Olympic medal because of his country's boycott, Steve Scott was annoyed at Ovett's decision to withdraw from a mile race in California. His 3000m defeat to Ovett the previous week made him look forward to gaining revenge and when he heard Ovett's decision not to run, he remarked, 'I expected it. He's very weird about who he runs against. He's just a talker.' Scott front-ran to an impressive 3:53.1 victory ahead of Eamonn Coghlan who commented, 'Ovett wouldn't have beaten Scott in that race.'

After returning home to an easy 800m win in Cwbran, Ovett fired the first shots as he and Coe jostled for a psychological advantage before Moscow. Organisers of the Philips Night of Athletics Meeting at Crystal Palace, four days later, announced that Ovett had switched from running the 800m to the Bannister Mile, which Coe had entered. Nobody thought for a minute that Coe would accept the challenge, but it served its intended purpose of annoying him.

Coe issued a statement to the media to diffuse speculation. 'I would appreciate the opportunity to race against Steve Ovett,' he said, 'but both the AAA and Ovett are well aware that any world-class athlete programmes his season to be at a racing peak at certain planned times.

'I am not at this moment attuned to run a race at near record schedule which might be misleading, not to say injurious, to one or both of us. Steve Ovett has never in the past been prepared to run in a race which did not suit his purpose and has been known to manipulate the field for his races.

'I believe it is wrong of him and the AAA, besides being unfair to the public, to contrive a race between us at short notice at this time. I am as eager to race against the best opposition as he is and have always sought it, and I look forward to racing Ovett when I am ready.'

Ovett thus won the Bannister mile, from Steve Cram, while Coe switched to Ovett's original event, the 800m. Ovett had won the first mental battle, but Coe's annoyance was obvious in the Crystal Palace press-box after the two races. 'I was annoyed at Ovett but the situation got out of hand,' he said, 'there was connivance. It was not the sort of game that should be played at this stage. I was annoyed that I had to rupture an agreement (to run in the Bannister Mile).'

Four days later Ovett attempted to force a confrontation once again, at the Inter Counties Championships in Birmingham. Ovett made a last minute move to represent Sussex in the mile. Coe had been selected to run for Yorkshire in the four lap event, but switched to the 800m, winning impressively in 1:45.5, while in the end Ovett didn't bother turning up for the mile. Coe added further scorching 800m times to his pre-Games 'armoury': 1:45.0 in the AAA versus Loughborough University match and on 11th June he ran 1:44.7 — the fastest two-lap time in the world so far in 1980 — in winning the Northern Championships at Hull.

With less than two months left until they flew out to Moscow, Coe began to counter this psychological offensive by attempting to shift some of the pressures of being favourite for the 1500m on to Ovett. In a *Daily Mail* interview he said, 'Taking into account Steve's collection of 1500m times and his long experience at the distance, how could you make me favourite? I've only run one 1500m in four years. I've only broken 3 minutes 40 seconds once. My best before the world record last year was 3 minutes 43 seconds. That's still my second best 1500m time.'

Coe did, however, concede that he had the best chance of winning the 800m and named four rivals as bigger threats than Ovett. And, talking about their rivalry, he said, 'I respect Steve as a fine runner. I hope he feels the same about me. That's how it should be. I don't always understand his way of going about things, but on the track that's irrelevant. I'm looking forward to meeting him whatever he chooses to run in Moscow.

'Steve and I haven't said more than a few sentences to each other in three years and then never about athletics. But is that surprising? How often do we meet? We live 250 miles apart. When one country has two outstanding runners in the same event it's only natural that the media create a rivalry. It's not a bad thing. The sport must benefit by the interest it generates.'

Ovett took up the initiative once again by leaving the decision about competing in Moscow until the last minute saying, 'I think anybody with a conscience must always weigh things up to the last possible date ... I am not sure one way or the other ... I hope to come to the right decision in the end.'

Steve claimed that he first considered missing the Games, because of the Russian invasion of Afghanistan, when he decided not to receive an athletics award from Prince Philip — President of the BAAB — at Buckingham Palace. He explained his decision not to attend the ceremony in a letter to David Shaw: 'I feel that due to the present climate following statements made by our nation's Government it would be unwise for me, an athlete, to attend a function which could involve the Royal Family in any controversial publicity at this time.'

Fears that Ovett and Coe would not meet each other after all, however, were never really in doubt. He had geared four years of training three times each day towards the Moscow Olympics and his parents had booked their flight tickets months earlier. His eventual decision to face Coe in both the 800m and the 1500m therefore came as no great surprise.

But his desire to gain the mental 'edge' over Coe before Moscow continued to obsess him. He clocked 3:33.3 for the 1500m at the Talbot Games on 27th June, when bad pacemaking spoilt his world record attempt. Despite the fast time, something seemed to be lacking in Ovett's performance. Steve Cram, the nineteen-year-old Tyneside runner who pressed his claims for Olympic selection by chasing Ovett right to the tape, summed up what many observers thought when he said, 'I think someone will beat Steve this year. He doesn't seem to have that little bit of zap he has had in the past'.

Ovett, however, gave those who were prepared to write off his Olympic chances plenty to think about in Oslo four days later, when he and Coe played the leading roles in one of the greatest evenings in British athletics history. First on the stage was Coe, setting a world 1000m record of 1:13.4 — after he had resisted Ovett's efforts to appear in the same race. The angular featured student set off on his lap of honour as a holder of four world records, but Ovett — warming up outside the stadium — was aiming to make him settle for three again within the next hour.

Dave Warren led the mile field through the first lap in 55 and 800m in 1:53.8 before leaving Ovett out in front on his own. He judged the pace to perfection, crossing the line 0.2 inside Coe's record; his time of 3:48.8 would have left Roger Bannister some 70 metres behind. Steve Cram further illustrated the progress made since the heady days of the mid-fifties by clocking 3:53.8 in second place to clinch the third British 1500m spot in the Olympics.

But it was Ovett's blistering performance which stole the show. Even David Shaw had a good word for the Brighton man's run, pointing out, 'It just shows that it would have been completely wrong to jump to the conclusion that not everything was right with his form in the Talbot Games.' Former Olympic 5000m silver medalist Gordon Pirie went further in his praise. 'He's the best runner Britain's ever had, no question,' he told Patrick Collins of the London *Evening News*. 'There's only one way he'll be beaten. You'd have to get close enough to him to trip him up.' After further considering his comments Pirie added, 'Getting close might be a problem'.

Ovett was naturally delighted with his run. 'One of my

big goals this season was to take this world record from Seb,' he said, adding, 'it tasted terrific.' After resisting further moves for a civic reception in Brighton, Ovett returned to Oslo on 15th July in an attempt to claim Coe's 1500m record. His world record appetite had become insatiable as he pushed his endeavours to gain a psychological advantage over Coe to their limits.

Trying to gain the offensive in this stopwatch warfare was fair enough, but many observers claimed that Ovett was stretching his form hard and dangerously far so soon before his ultimate test in Moscow — the Olympic 800m heats were only nine days away.

As the *Daily Mail* athletics correspondent Neil Wilson commented, 'Never can an Olympic favourite have put his reputation and his confidence on the line so few days before his Olympic ordeal.' It was not merely gamesmanship that prompted Ovett to run. He wanted to prove that the absentees in Moscow would have stood little chance.

Steve Scott, Craig Masback, Thomas Wessinghage, John Walker and Eamonn Coghlan were in the field. And it became a classic confrontation following Scott's pre-race prediction to the Press that he was going to defeat Ovett. 'I've been waiting a long time for this,' said the burly American. 'I've said all year I'll meet him any time, any place, but everywhere I turned out he went missing. Ovett said a lot of things in the past which I haven't liked and I've got a long memory.'

Scott consequently made a bold front-running attempt to draw the sting out of Ovett's finishing kick. With 100m remaining, he led Ovett and Wessinghage but Ovett left both men standing in the home straight. Glancing round at Scott he waved to the crowd as he slowed down through the tape. Incredibly, his time was 3:32.1 — exactly the same as Coe's world record. A Hollywood scriptwriter couldn't have dreamed up a more tantalising finishing touch for the build-up to the Ovett–Coe showdown.

Ovett gave his reasons for running so close to the Games

as the need to defeat a strong field. 'I still needed inspiration,' he said. 'In this performance I discovered that my body would okay my will. It was all right and went more or less as I hoped, but I don't think it was all that wonderful.' Back home in Sheffield, Coe commented, 'It's becoming quite a thing now — it's a little bit theatrical really.'

It certainly was. And, as Ovett and Coe made their final preparations for the trip to Moscow, Britain was swept by a form of Olympic fever it had never experienced before. The sports pages were filled with predictions about the outcome of the 'big clash'. John Rodda of the *Guardian* plumped for Coe in the 800m and Ovett in the 1500m and David Miller of the *Daily Express* took Coe to win both, while the reigning Olympic 1500m champion John Walker was in no doubt. 'There is no comparison,' he said. 'Coe will win both.'

The general consensus of opinion was that Coe would win the 800m with little difficulty while the 1500m would be one of the closest run Olympic finals of all time. Such was their rivals' fear that the gold and silver 1500m medals were already bound for Brighton and Sheffield, that they moved up to the 5000m — despite the presence of Miruts Yifter and Lasse Viren. Eamonn Coghlan, who had finished fourth in the 1976 Olympic 1500m and second in the 1978 European championships, and Commonwealth Games champion Dave Moorcroft both plumped for the twelve and a half lap race. And, but for his country's boycott, Thomas Wessinghage would have joined them.

After Ovett had refused to speak to the Press for five years (apart from an interview with the *Daily Star* in November 1978), the *Sunday People* carried three exclusive interviews with Ovett during the Games. 'So much has been said by other people that I feel it's time to have the truth out in the open,' he told interviewer David Barnes in the first article, published as the British team flew out to Moscow. On the subject of his rivalry with Coe, he said, 'It's true that we're not the best of friends, but neither are we enemies. We are rivals. It's as simple as that. We are not friends because we have not grown up together in the sport. We live in different parts of the country and Seb has only been around about a year. I have developed with other athletes. I just don't know Seb well enough to get into long conversations. But, of course, there is more to it.'

'It's true that we consciously avoid each other at public receptions. Seb knows the very good reason for that as well as I do. It's because a lot of people follow us around on occasions like that. They're waiting for us to meet. We know we wouldn't be natural. We'd be asked to smile at each other for pictures. People would ask who was the better runner, who would beat the other. It would be too embarrassing. We don't need the hassle as we get on with preparing for the big events.'

Discussing his Olympic chances, Ovett remarked, 'I've got a 50 per cent chance of winning the 800m and 90 per cent chance of winning the 1500m. I don't really like the 800m. I've only raced two or three times in the last couple of years ... I'm in the 800m because I'm in Moscow and I do want to win it. But the race is over too quickly for me. The 1500m is the one I'm really prepared for. It's the one I want. Steve Ovett is a miler.'

Coe flew out to Moscow with the official British party, two days before Ovett, and reacted sharply to some of Ovett's comments at a massive press conference. 'Has he got a crystal ball?' remarked Coe. 'I've never thought percentages have anything to do with athletics. But that is Steve. I am pleased he is so confident. I respect anybody who puts on running shoes and goes out to run. Steve does that and he is a very fine athlete with it. I have thought more about Steve Ovett in twenty minutes here, than I do in a month'.

One particular comment in Ovett's article hurt Coe deeply. Labelling him a 'Programmed runner', Ovett said, 'From getting up in the morning to going to bed, Seb is programmed. It's almost scientific. I'm the opposite. I make up my mind at the last minute, depending on how I feel and what I need.' Coe countered the claims by saying, 'At the level we're running, natural talent has to be the major part of athletics. It isn't quantifiable, but talent comes above natural science. I don't think I am any more programmed than any other athlete'.

Ovett arrived in Moscow just two days before the 800m heats, courting his 'different from the rest' image. He was the only athlete to shun the compulsory British uniform, choosing a tongue-in-cheek pin-striped suit instead: he was ready for the showdown. One recalled Ovett's answer to a question Mel Watman had put to him in *Athletics Weekly* the previous year — 'No, I won't be bothered if I win an Olympic gold medal. I sometimes go to schools and see a lot of kids who can't run, can hardly walk, and to be blessed with the ability to run is enough. Olympic golds are secondary really.'

In front of 90,000 people Ovett and Coe eased through the heats and semi-finals. Coe was the clear favourite. His fluency had been impressive and when Olaf Beyer fell over in his semi-final it seemed that nothing could stop Coe winning the 800m final. Nobody doubted Ovett's racing power but his best two-lap time was two seconds behind Coe's world record. It was considered a secondary event for the Brighton runner and the American magazine *Track and Field News* didn't even rate him in the top six in their pre-Games prediction.

On Saturday 26th July CTNBAH OBETT, CEBACTBRN KOY and the six other finalists lined up for the 1980 Olympic 800m final. The huge crowd in the Lenin Stadium held their breath. Throughout the world a vast television audience sat glued to their sets. This was the showdown *everybody* wanted to see ...

After it was all over an air of muted disbelief filled the Lenin Stadium. The most eagerly awaited foot race of the twentieth century had been and gone. Around the red track bounded an ebullient, balding figure in a Great Britain vest, numbered 279. Brushing past Russian guards, he ran to the British contingent of supporters down the back straight and gesticulated triumphantly.

Above his head, the electronic scoreboard flashed the result of the 1980 Olympic 800 metres final against the striking back-cloth of a typically steely Russian evening sky:

1.	Steven Ovett	GB	1:45.4
2.	Sebastian Coe	GB	1:45.9
3.	Nikolai Kirov	USSR	1:46.0
4.	Agberto Guimaraes	BRAZIL	1:46.2
5.	Andreas Busse	GDR	1:46.9
6.	Detlef Wagenknecht	GDR	1:47.0
7.	Jose Marajo	FRANCE	1:47.3
8.	David Warren	GB	1:49.3

Coe winced as he shook hands with Ovett on the rostrum. All the hours of gruelling training reaped their just rewards as Ovett collected the gold medal. Less than two minutes had decided two years debate.

Coe had been content to spectate behind the pack when Ovett found himself boxed in by the East Germans, as Kirov and Guimaraes took the pace on the first lap. The Brazilian led at the bell in the slow time of 54.55 with Ovett battling his way out of trouble and Coe content to watch the fists fly from afar. Suddenly, the race began to explode into action.

Warren took the lead and Kirov chased after him. Ovett sensed it was time to move and hared after them down the back straight. With 200m left to fight for the precious medals Kirov took over from the fading Warren with Ovett a stride behind. Coe, who had been hopelessly detached down the back straight, was still ten metres down and battled hard to keep in touch with the leaders around the final bend. Although he was within striking distance of Ovett as they entered the final 100m, he had used up valuable speed.

Ovett rocketed away to as comfortable a gold medal as

was ever won in the home straight of an Olympic final. Coe passed Guimareas 40m out and pipped Kirov for the silver medal a couple of strides from the line.

Ovett's facial expression displayed a mixture of surprise and elation as he raised his index finger to send his now familiar 'I love you' message to his girlfriend Rachel Waller who was watching on television at home. He judged the race, that he didn't expect to win, to perfection, whereas Coe left himself too much to do in the final furlong. As Dave Warren remarked, 'I am surprised at Coe running like that when he can run a 1:44 race on the Loughborough cinders.'

Although it was a bruising affair, it was still a memorable race. One Dutch TV commentator called it '... a race without history, a race without soul'. The media had confidently expected Coe to win but he had been unable even to get near to Ovett. The great confrontation had turned into a one horse affair; the watching world was stunned by the fact that even with 80m left Coe had failed to make an impression on the race.

'I know I threw it away on the second lap,' said the bitterly disappointed Loughborough Student. 'I went into the race feeling I was capable of coping with anything that might be thrown at me, but when they broke I didn't have the speed of thought or movement necessary. Don't ask me why. Some days you perform well, others you don't. I didn't respond when Kirov made the break at the front on the second back straight, and that fatal error cost me the race.

'I must have compounded more cardinal sins of middle distance running in the space of one and a half minutes than I've done in a lifetime. What a race to choose. My big mistake was losing contact around the final bend. When I had sorted out the problems there were a couple of guys too far ahead up the straight. And Steve was one of them. This time I ran badly, next time who knows?'

After a night of celebration among the Ovett family in the Russian capital Steve gave an interview on ITV.

Interviewer Adrian Metcalfe suggested that Ovett was now a 'megastar'. Ovett countered laughingly, 'No I can't see it, honestly. It's like last night. I came back and put my medal on the table and said to Harry (Wilson), "It just goes to prove that any idiot can become an Olympic Champion."'

Talking about the tough race behind him, Ovett admitted, 'If anyone was guilty of doing more than a fair share of pushing, it was probably me. I can be called the worst of the bunch, but I honestly believe that everyone ran a fair race. People were wearing half inch spikes and, if anyone gets close to you, you fend them off because they are dangerous. It looks as if you're pushing everyone everywhere, but it's really a matter of safety precautions.'

Ovett, nevertheless, had the gold medal in his pocket and it was time for Race of the Century Mark II. Said Ovett, 'The big problem for me now is to relax and get back to basic training and get back to preparing for three hard races which — after you've won a gold — is very difficult. There are other runners who are now determined to prove that the 800m was in no way a true reflection of their calibre in the 1500m. Seb is obviously going to be there and I've a great deal of respect for Straub.'

The pundits were now heavily backing Ovett to clinch the title of the world's greatest ever middle distance runner by winning the 1500m. Strangely enough Ovett's heat win (3:36.8) ahead of Straub was to have a significant bearing on the final. The newly-crowned Olympic 800m champion was made to work hard to keep his unbeaten 1500m/mile record intact, the East German management team had instructed Straub to 'stretch' Ovett in this race as part of their long term plan to help their top athlete upset the odds in the final. Coe, meanwhile, was content to finish behind Italy's Vittorio Fontanella in his heat (in a time of 3:40.1).

Coe showed that he could barge his way out of trouble as well as Ovett in his 3:39.34 semi-final victory over Straub. A fluent and strong-looking Ovett won his semi-final in 3:43.1 with Steve Cram only just managing to qualify for the final in his wake. It was the Brighton man's 45th

Top: Even as a thirteen-year-old, training in Brighton's Preston Park, the raking leg cadence and flicking back left hand were an integral part of Steve Ovett's distinctive running style (REG HOOK)
Bottom: Training with Lesley Kiernan in Preston Park, 1973 (REG HOOK)

Alberto Juantorena (217) leads Ovett (375) and the late Ivo Van Damme (103 in the 1976 Olympic 800m semi-final. Juantorena went on to collect the gold medal in the final and Van Damme took the silver, while Ovett finished a disappointing fifth (GEORGE HERRINGSHAW)

Top: Training on the Brighton seafront in 1974 (TONY DUFFY)
Bottom: The people's choice – receiving the 1978 BBC Sports Personality of the Year trophy from Prince Charles (BBC TV)

)pposite: Ovett conveys, to his parents sitting in the stands, his surprise at
eating Coe but still losing in the 1978 European Championships 800m final
ΛIKE STREET)
op: United in defeat – Ovett embraces Sebastian Coe after they have both
een surprisingly defeated by East German Olaf Beyer in the 1978 European
hampionships 800m (MARK SHEARMAN)
ottom: With coach Harry Wilson, 1979 (PRESS ASSOCIATION)

Top: 'Any idiot can become an Olympic Champion' Ovett blasts to victory in the 1980 Olympic 800m final as Coe has his hands full in pipping Russia's Nikolai Kirov to the silver medal (GEORGE HERRINGSHAW)
Bottom: 'What happened to you?' A rare moment of communication between Seb and Steve on the rostrum in Moscow, as Ovett waits to receive the 800m gold medal (GEORGE HERRINGSHAW)

›p: With future wife Rachel in Oslo, 1981, the day before Ovett was beaten
y his pacemaker Tom Byers (MARK SHEARMAN)
›ottom: Greeting disabled fans after his win in the 1979 Coca Cola Mile
EORGE HERRINGSHAW)

Dubbed a 'genial artist' by his former art master, Steve Ovett displays some of his work in the garden of his parents' home in Brighton (MIKE STREET)

consecutive 1500m/mile win and led Neil Wilson of the *Daily Mail* to comment, 'It will take a superhuman effort to beat Ovett.' The only sports writer who believed Coe was capable of ending Ovett's winning streak was the co-writer of his autobiography David Miller of the *Daily Express*. Coe himself, was in no doubt about the enormity of the task confronting him.

'This is unquestionably going to be probably the toughest race I shall ever face mentally and physically, whether or not I carry on to the 1984 Olympics,' he said. 'I believe I'm fast enough to win but I will have to run not only a punishing last lap but must eliminate the mistakes I made last week. There is no reason why I shouldn't.'

This time, the confrontation had a double edge. If Ovett won, he would be hailed as unquestionably the greater runner of the two. Faced with being dismissed in British athletics history as a 'clockwork' runner devoid of a racing edge, Coe had to make that 'superhuman effort' to win and keep the debate 'open'.

Friday, 1st August was a day of intense interest and pressure in Moscow's Lenin Stadium. A measure of the race's significance was echoed in the fact that at least £75,000 was paid to advertise on TV immediately before and after the race — in the London area alone. Steve Cram, the third Briton in the final, takes up the pre-race story. 'I considered myself very privileged to be the only other British guy there to see what was happening. I went down to the stadium in the same car as Steve and Harry Wilson — Seb tends to be locked together with his father. I thought Steve would have been confident because of his 800m victory and his impressive form in the heats. But it was quite the opposite. He was talking about trying to win *a* medal, rather than *the* medal, which I didn't think was a very positive attitude to be going into such a race with. He kept asking Harry if Seb had arrived yet and was obviously very conscious of Seb.

'When we were warming up Steve said he was very tired and he looked it. In the waiting room, Seb was walking up and down the middle and Steve went up to him and tried to make conversation. At first, I thought Steve was trying to psych Seb out, but it was quite obviously nerves. Steve was trying to 'overcome' the tension by making conversation, but Seb just wasn't interested. It was quite funny, really. I thought they would be at opposite ends of the room eyeing one another up and avoiding contact, but it must have counted in the end. Steve obviously wasn't as hungry as Seb to win that gold medal.'

As the race unfolded, an unexpected element in the seemingly polarised battle began to emerge in the blue-vested shape of Jurgen Straub. The East German former steeplechaser led the nine man field through 400m in the leisurely time 61.7 with Coe and Ovett tucked in behind him. The positions remained unchanged on the second lap, which was even slower — 63.3. Straub was controlling the race from the front at his own pace, while Coe and Ovett were in ideal positions to cover any threatening moves.

The warm-up was over. Straub began his long 'kick' for home from 700m out, hoping that a sustained drive might take the sting out of Ovett and Coe's feared finishing bursts. It was a Godsend for Coe, who stuck to Straub's shoulder, with Ovett a further stride behind. Straub covered the 3rd lap in a blistering 54.2 seconds and set up the race for a classic final 300m. He still powered down the back straight, showing no signs of relenting, as the 'big two' struggled to keep in touch. With 200m left there were certainly only three men chasing the medals — Straub, Coe and Ovett. Coe closed on Straub around the final turn, with Ovett's figure still looming menacingly on his shoulder.

Coming off the bend, Coe glanced over his right shoulder to check Ovett's position. Ovett's face held a relaxed expression: he seemed set for double gold. But a crucial difference lay in Coe's expression. Teeth gritted, he kicked past Straub and then moved up another gear to make sure of the gold medal. It was a special 'double kick' which Coe had been perfecting in training and against which Ovett was powerless to respond. Straub's gritty determination held off Ovett in the closing strides to collect a well-earned silver medal. Ovett's determination having waned to such an extent that a silver milk bottle top would have been as acceptable as any of the 'lesser' medals.

It was an enthralling race. The three leading protagonists had been in their ideal positions 100m from home, but the deciding factor was quite clearly the result of the 800m. Ovett's will to win had been blunted by the gold medal that was already packed in his suitcase while Coe's expected two lap defeat allied a steely racing edge and overpowering determination to his undoubted speed.

Had that psychological advantage not been there, it would have been a tighter race in the home straight, but athletics is as much about the mind as physical conditioning. Nobody could deny Coe his deserved moment of glory. He had scaled the mental and physical heights to the pinnacle of athletic success within six days and brought the ideal result to the Ovett–Coe melodrama: a 1–1 draw, with two own goals. The predictions were turned on their heads as each man collected the gold medal the other had wanted but overall, the debate was still 'open'.

Shaking hands with Coe at the finish and smiling on the medal rostrum, Steve Ovett gained the world's respect with his sporting manner in defeat. He now looked drained and jaded but it took two almighty individual performances to halt his glorious unbeaten run. This time the scoreboard read:

1.	Sebastian Coe	GB	3:38.4
2.	Jurgen Straub	GDR	3:38.8
3.	Steven Ovett	GB	3:39.0
4.	Andreas Busse	GDR	3:40.2
5.	Vittario Fontanella	ITALY	3:40.4
6.	Jozef Plachy	CZECHOSLOVAKIA	3:40.7
7.	Jose Marajo	FRANCE	3:41.5
8.	Steven Cram	GB	3:42.0
9.	Dragan Zdravkovic	YUGOSLAVIA	3:43.1

'I was mentally well-prepared for the race,' said Coe, 'and I was doing what I do best — running, freely and uncluttered, thanks to Straub. I couldn't have wished for an easier run. There was no way I was going to be off the pace this time. I felt after I kicked that I had made some daylight straight away. I wasn't sure how much distance I had to spare over Steve at the end, but now I've seen it on video I'm surprised how far away he was. Steve's a magnificent athlete and I have sympathy for him. We wished each other well before the race and we're planning to have a few drinks together.'

Steve gave his views on the race to David Barnes in the *Sunday People*: 'I've never buckled under pressure before,' he said, 'but when you're standing on the Olympic line and the gun goes, you are completely alone. The pressure of that is immense. And it looks as though Seb buckled in the 800m and I did the same in the 1500m. I felt fine before the race and pretty comfortable into the last 150m. Just as we came off the curve I tried to sprint with Coe and Straub, but there was no power. I was a man with tired legs; I just didn't realise how tired I was. I'm as proud of my bronze as I am of my gold because I did my best.'

The sharing of defeat, victory and intense pressure in the sweltering cauldron of the Olympic Games brought Ovett and Coe closer together in Moscow. And Coe was in no doubt about the conclusions to be drawn from his experiences. 'There has been tremendous pressure on both of us here,' he told Cliff Temple in *The Sunday Times*, 'Steve and I agreed, when we were waiting together in the doping control room that the results here are more those of Olympic pressure than anything.

'Above all,' he added, 'it will have taken a lot of pressure off us both. We may be racing each other quite regularly during the next three or four years, but now the big confrontation is out of the way, it may never be the same again.'

Coe couldn't have been wider off the mark. After both men returned to their respective home towns and warm receptions, the pressure to produce a final result increased daily. The Olympic Games settled nothing. Islington sports promoter Frank Warren offered them 'more than anything they've been offered before' to turn professional and take part in a 'deciding' race, in return for which he would also underwrite £2,000,000 to the Cancer Research Campaign. But however tempting the offer, Ovett and Coe were not prepared to turn professional unless the rules of amateur competition were altered.

'The two of us are worth millions in world wide promotional terms,' said Ovett in the *Sunday People*. 'I can't speak for Seb, but it's true that if we turn professional it could drive a wedge into the amateur sport. But first I would like to think that amateur sport will change to keep us within its bounds.' His enthusiasm for such a clash was obvious in a BBC radio interview. 'The potential for us meeting again is phenomenal,' he said, 'it's what people want to see — just like an Ali–Foreman clash in boxing. But, as amateurs, we are not allowed to run for money, not even for something like Cancer Research. Certain rules of the IAAF need changing. They are too archaic.'

Nevertheless, it seemed likely that they would meet in an 'amateur' race when both accepted invitations from the IAAF to run in the Gillette Golden Mile at Crystal Palace on 25th August. All 17,000 tickets were snapped up weeks before the Bank Holiday Monday date. Such was the interest that Crystal Palace officials were forced to consider installing temporary seating and TV rights were sold to the USA, Japan and New Zealand.

Six days before the race, BAAB General Secretary David Shaw held a press conference and confirmed that both Ovett and Coe would be running. Ovett, said Shaw, 'would be running irrespective of who else would be competing' and Peter Coe had assured him that there were 'no problems' about Seb running. 'From our point of view, we are absolutely delighted,' concluded Shaw.

All was ready for the 'showdown' in a perfect setting: the two most famous British runners fighting over the British mile in front of a packed bank holiday British crowd at the home of British athletics. Ovett was made evens favourite by the bookmakers with Coe at 11–10 and 10–1 others as the British public anticipated a sporting occasion to rival the Boat Race, the Cup Final, Wimbledon and the Grand National rolled into one. The 'peripheral' events associated with such great sporting occasions helped to build up the tension, but it was the four lap race itself which held the imagination. Ovett won the first Golden Mile in Tokyo in 1978. Coe took the title the following year in a world record time. The 1980 Golden Mile was all set to settle the question of which was the best runner once and for all.

But all that was Golden didn't glitter. Two days after the press conference, it was David Shaw's thankless task to tell the waiting world that there would be no 'clash of the century' after all. Coe suddenly cut his season short because of a trapped sciatic nerve. Amid suspicions that the Loughborough student was using his long term injury as an excuse, Coe said, 'The pity about this year's Golden Mile is that it has come at a difficult time, when many of the athletes are tired. But, even so, I am particularly sorry that my back trouble has recurred.

'Even if I had been fit to run, I was unhappy that British athletics was gaining almost none of the financial benefit,' he continued. 'Steve, I, and the others were in effect running to fill the pockets of TV companies and advertising agencies.' London-based sports promoters West Nally, who stood to gain the lion's share of the money generated by the clash, lost $50,000 when NBC pulled out of a deal the moment Coe's withdrawal was announced.

So in what kind of situation *was* Coe prepared to face Ovett? 'I don't want to turn professional,' he said. 'And I believe the full financial potential of a mile race between Steve and me on British soil, properly organised and sold to television in America and elsewhere, directly and not through an agent, should be tapped for the finances of the sport in Britain. British athletics needs the money and I am sure that Steve, who has always said how his main concern is for the grass roots of the sport, would agree to such a race at the right time.'

But Coe's words couldn't dampen the widespread disappointment at the cancellation of the clash. In the battery of post-Olympic meetings both he and Ovett had been releasing nervous energy which had built up in Moscow on the running tracks of Europe. At the Crystal Palace IAC/Coca Cola meeting Coe impressively won the 800m in 1:45.9 and Ovett ran a brilliant 4995 metres. Always well placed in the 5000m, Steve 'kicked' for home in the last 100m. As he drew clear, he waved to the crowd and eased down in anticipation of the finishing line, having fended off a burst from Irishman John Tracey.

The inevitable happened as Ovett's critic saw what they had been waiting to see for a long time. With arms aloft Ovett was pipped on the line, Tracey being given the photo-finish verdict. Only an Irishman, wearing the number 13, could have done it but the feeling was that Ovett had at last received what his home straight antics deserved. Nevertheless, this time there was a good reason for his waving (see chapter seven) and his time of 13:27.9 gave further evidence of his potential at the twelve and a half lap distance. This was emphasised four days later when he clocked 13:32.0 in defeating Wilson Waigwa and Filbert Bayi in a 5000m race at Budapest.

Before his back injury worsened, Coe came close to breaking the 1500m record he and Ovett shared by clocking 3:32.2 in Zurich. The following evening Coe moved on to Viarregio in Italy and was beaten by America's Don Paige in a 800m race which turned out to be his final race of the season. Ovett, meanwhile, failed with a 1500m world record attempt in Lausanne and in a mile attempt in Brussels.

The Coe-less Golden Mile was naturally surrounded by an air of anti-climax. Ovett did no more than was necessary to fend of the challenge by Scott in the home straight in what was considered a disappointing race, but the measure of Ovett's talent was echoed in his winning time — 'only' 3:52.84! There was also the fact that he comfortably defeated all the world's top milers apart from the injured Coe and Straub, whose invitation was turned down by the East German authorities.

It was, however, not a wholly memorable day for Ovett. Disgruntled after the failure of his latest track attack on Ovett, Steve Scott launched another verbal assault on his elusive English adversary. 'Many of the things Steve does work against the sport,' Scott told Bob Harris of Thomson Regional Newspapers. 'Things like waving at the crowd off the final bend and refusing to talk to the Press are in my mind, negatives. Others, like myself and Seb Coe, are doing our best to promote the sport. I have no criticism of Steve as an athlete — he is tremendous. But, in his position, he should not hurt athletics. You cannot help comparing him with Coe, who is easier to get on with and doesn't put himself up on a cloud.'

Ovett's answer to this latest criticism came on the track in Koblenz, West Germany on Wednesday, 27th August, where he once again tried to break the 1500m record. Wolverhampton runner Garry Cook made the pace, taking Ovett, Thomas Wessinghage and Harold Hudak through 400m in 55.5 and 800m in 1:53.00. Wessinghage took over on the crucial third lap to pass 1200m in 2:49.6, the same time as when Ovett equalled the record in Oslo. However, the German doctor wasn't in the race just to set up the record for Ovett. He wanted to claim it himself in front of his 'home' crowd and was attempting to draw the sting out of Ovett's sprint finish *à al* Straub, with a prolonged 'kick'. Only in the home straight did Ovett manage to edge past to break the tape only a stride ahead of his old adversary.

The competition, however, was sufficiently stiff for the Brighton runner to reduce the record by 7/10th of a second (3:31.4). Wessinghage's bold efforts were rewarded with a personal best time of 3:31.58, which was also inside the record, while his relatively unknown patriot Hudak became the third fastest metric miler in history by improving his personal best from 3:36.1 to 3:31.96.

'The main reason the record went was that Wessinghage stayed so close,' said an elated Ovett after the race. 'Now it should be possible to beat 3:30 next year. But there are only two men who can do it — myself and Wessinghage.' Ovett went on to end his season with a mile win in the AAA centenary championships at Crystal Palace.

It had been a memorable season. Ovett had won Olympic gold and bronze medals, broken the world's two most prized records and established himself as the greatest miler/metric miler of all time (by stretching his unbeaten record to 45 consecutive races) and once again displayed his 5000m potential. The AAA the readers of *Athletics Weekly*, the staff of *Athletics Monthly* and even the Athletics Writers Association all responded by voting him 'Athlete of the Year'.

After pusuing his charity interests in Sussex (see chapter seven), Ovett took a well-earned holiday in Los Angeles with Rachel. Despite the 'drawn' Olympic confrontation, Ovett had beaten Coe at his own record breaking game to gain the upper hand in their rivalry. And the agencies, TV promoters, Press and public looked forward to the big question being resolved once and for all the following season.

Six

Postal Chess

1981 was in many respects a watershed in Steve Ovett's life and in his running career. He broke his strong parental ties by marrying Rachel Waller, thus creating a more independent personal future. He parted company with Brighton and Hove AC, causing a great deal of ill-feeling among the south coast athletic fraternity in the process. And his training partner Matt Paterson took a more prominent role in Steve's coaching as Harry Wilson's influence began to wane.

And despite having another memorable season on the running track itself, he didn't quite manage to build on his 1980 season as much as he had hoped. This led many observers and fellow athletes to conclude that after eight years in the international athletics limelight (three more than Coe), he had finally reached the point of no improvement. Ovett himself admitted, 'If I don't improve next season I'm going to get wiped out. It's as simple as that.'

In March he ended an eleven year association with Brighton and Hove Athletic Club, in which time he had developed from an awkward-looking sprinter into arguably the world's greatest-ever middle distance runner. Ovett joined his training partner Matt Paterson, a former club captain and committee member, in forming a rival Brighton club, which they named Phoenix Athletics Club. Paterson had coached many of the club's promising young runners and when the club was inundated with young hopefuls, following Ovett's Olympic success, Paterson felt that 'the club has simply not fulfilled its obligation to those youngsters who have joined'.

Tony Tilbury's attempt to bring Ovett closer within the club structure, by suggesting he should train with the club captain, worked against the club in the long run. 'Paterson was drawn further and further away from the club activities,' says Tilbury. Essentially, the quarrel was between Paterson and the club committee.

As the President, Reg Hook point out: 'I think Steve played a very minor part in the split. He left the club primarily through his loyalty to Matt. We received a really nice letter of resignation from Steve, saying he'd enjoyed his time at the club and wishing us every success in the future. The club has no beef with Steve. We didn't see him that much when he was a member anyway. We presented him with a painting of the South Downs at a special "do" we put on for him at the Brighton Centre in October 1980. Locally, he's still worshipped by all of the kids and held in a great deal of respect by the adults.'

After leaving his parents' home and moving in with Rachel, Steve rested from training for two months and in April he ran his first race for seven months — his longest absence since suffering from glandular fever in 1974. Fears that the long lay-off, together with a leg injury, would affect Ovett's 1981 season were comprehensively dispelled when he travelled to the ancient Northern Italian market town of Viegevano to take part in the 'Golden Shoe' race. Ovett led from gun to tape in the 7.5km race around the town's cobbled streets.

Dampened by a chilling Italian rainstorm but warmed by the sound of church bells, car horns, bugles and trumpets, he left Olympic steeplechaser Alberto Cova twelve seconds behind in a race that Coe had won in 1980. 'I will look forward to facing Coe here next season,' said Ovett at a post race press conference, in which he declared his aim for the season was to win the World Cup 1500m in Rome.

Ovett's controversial opening to 1981 continued when he launched a frustrated attack on Coe for 'avoiding' him. 'It's not probable that we will meet,' he told the *Daily Mail*'s Neil Wilson. 'Don't ask me why. Just phone Coe. It is not a question of me escaping from him. We do not meet because Seb does not make it possible. It's unfortunate. I have never said no to running against him anywhere. Both times I have said I wanted to race him he has said no.' Coe reacted by calling Ovett's claims 'a joke' and reiterated that he would not plan his athletics career with anyone other than himself in mind.

As the track season swung into action, Ovett ran into trouble once again. No less than 200 of Britain's top athletes boycotted the UK championships in Antrim, because of what the historians call 'the Irish Problem'. Running in his first major track race of the season, Ovett won the 1500m title in 3:42.80, ahead of Frank Clements. But it was events away from the running track which hit the headlines.

David Shaw had not been informed of Ovett's decision to run in the province until shortly before the 1500m heats. Having never been a fan of Ovett's, Shaw was annoyed at Ovett's last minute decision to run, which delighted the 5000 crowd. 'This was not a last minute thing,' claimed Shaw. 'Something has been going on all week and I am uptight about it. I am not going to say no to Ovett taking part because we have said all along we would accept last minute entries.'

'But if he had announced his decision earlier it would have given a strong lead to many athletes who look up to him. There are too many people pulling strings and too many people in this sport who are playing at God. It is turning athletics into a shambles.'

Ovett claimed he had made a decision to run at Antrim the day before the meeting and that a delayed shuttle to Belfast had caused him to arrive only 90 minutes before the 1500m heats. He was so annoyed at Shaw's stinging outburst that he attended a British press conference for the first time in six years. 'I think it is rather farcical of Shaw to criticise me because I am here to help athletics,' said Ovett.

'He seems more interested in the political side than in the sport in general.'

When asked if there was a rift between himself and Shaw, Ovett replied: 'I think before you can have a rift, there has to be communication. The last time David Shaw phoned me was over two years ago ... we rarely speak. The last time we spoke was when the Board (BAAB) tried to ban me after competing in Nijmegen.'

Since that battle for supremacy in British athletics, centred around the question of whether the athletes, the BAAB, or the AAA could dictate where athletes could or could not run, an enormous gulf had emerged between all parties; or as Ovett's friend and adviser Andy Norman, himself an AAA official, called it, 'a war of attrition' had developed. Ovett concluded his press conference by saying, 'I think I do my best for athletics and I never let anybody down. Ask the people here if they think my coming was worthwhile. That's the main thing.'

Shaw half apologised for his outburst a few days later, saying, 'It was foolish of me. It was a measure of the pressure on the event which had built up on me.' But he stuck to the main body of his argument: 'What I said was not wrong. And what Steve said of me in reply was ludicrously unfair. If I had not worked so hard he would not have been able to run in Northern Ireland.' This particular chapter in what was developing into a personal battle between Shaw and Ovett thereupon closed, but another one was to start later in the season.

Attention at last began to return to the track. And in the Philips Night of Athletics meeting at Crystal Palace on 3rd June, the world's two hottest running properties once again stole the headlines. Ovett braved a sore throat to win the 3000m from the stalwart Belgian distance runner Emile Puttemans, while Coe clocked the storming time of 1:44.06 in winning the 800m.

But it was the Sheffield man's turn to face off-the-track controversy. Neil Allen of the *New Standard* alleged that 'a satellite of the Mark McCormack organisation', who boast

Coe's father as one of their clients, had requested over £7,000 for Coe's appearance in a race near Paris later that month. The Coes refuted the allegations and a week later Seb overshadowed the inevitable speculation by setting astonishing figures of 1:41.72 in breaking his world 800m record in Italy.

Meanwhile Ovett's rift with the BAAB opened again. He and Olympic 100m champion Allan Wells refused to run for Britain in the match against West Germany and Poland at Crystal Palace on 23rd and 24th June. Although the BAAB had been informed of the two athletes' plans for the season in January, Shaw implied that if they didn't run they would risk being dropped for the forthcoming Europa Cup semi-final in Helsinki. In view of the fact that Coe had been given permission to miss the Crystal Palace meeting to run in Paris, both Ovett and Wells were incensed that they were being singled out. 'I cannot be expected to race like a robot,' said Wells. 'That meeting was never included in my programme and the BAAB know it.'

Shaw hinted that he would vote to 'drop' the two Olympic champions for the Helsinki match at the selection committee meeting. 'I will make my views clear, but I am only one man on a commitee,' said the BAAB General Secretary. But Ovett and Wells were worth valuable points in Britain's tough battle to qualify for the Europa Cup final and the committee decided they couldn't afford to do without them. The week ended with Ovett hoping to lower his 1500m record at the Bislett Games in Oslo.

At the last minute Tom Byers, a 26-year-old American student from Eugene, Oregon, who ranked sixth in his country in the metric mile, was called in to pacemake for Ovett. Byers set off at a phenomenal speed, leaving Ovett, Scott, Cram and Wessinghage 40m adrift at 800m. Over the next 100m, it became clear that Ovett was in danger of being beaten as Byers stretched his lead to nearly 80m. 'They must have thought I would drop dead,' said Byers, who was still 70m clear at the bell.

Ovett hared around the final 300m and made up all but

4m of the deficit but just couldn't catch the American 'rabbit' who clocked 3:39.01, 0.52 of a second ahead of Ovett. It was only Ovett's second 1500m defeat in four years and his only consolation was his victory over the rest of the talented field. It was one of the most unusual races on the European circuit, where the middle distance wins of Ovett and Coe have, despite the intense interest and excitement they invariably generate, often been predictable and stereotyped. Ovett appreciated the novelty of his defeat. 'We all ran like a load of hacks,' he said, still scratching his head after the race.

Ovett returned to Scandinavia on 4th July to help Britain in their Europa Cup Semi-Final. Suffering from toothache (his infected gums cause him frequent trouble) and short of both sleep and training all week, he won the 1500m in 3:46.47 after a sprint finish up the home straight. Further individual victories from Allan Wells (100m and 200m), Seb Coe (800m), Barry Smith (5000m), Keith Stock (Pole Vault), Roy Mitchell (Long Jump) and wins in both relays earned Britain their first outright win since the competition's inception in 1965 — and ahead of the mighty Soviet Union.

With team duty out of the way, Ovett and Coe proceeded in their quest to re-write the record books. Coe missed Ovett's 1500m record by 56/100ths of a second by recording 3:31.95 — only Ovett and Wessinghage had run faster — in Stockholm. And Ovett attacked the same record 24 hours later in front of 20,000 spectators in Milan's Arena Napoleon.

His tactics of waiting until 300m out before 'kicking' once again cost Ovett the record: his time was 3:31.95, precisely the same as the time (to 1/100th of a second) Coe had recorded the previous evening. While Coe's run had been universally hailed by the Press, the headline 'Ovett Slump' in one national newspaper greeted the Brighton runner's equal third fastest metric mile of all time — an indication of the Press's contrasting regard for the two men, the high standards Ovett had set and the fact that the knives were well and truly poised for the slightest slip from Steve.

The world record seeking roadshow moved on to the familiar stage of Oslo's Bislett Stadium (called the 'Upton Park of Scandinavian athletics' by Norman Fox of *The Times*) for the Dulux Oslo Games on 11th July. Ovett and the cream of the world's middle distance runners were pencilled in for the Dream Mile, for which ABC had paid £150 a second for the exclusive television rights.

Feeling that he was ready to face Ovett, Coe asked the organisers if he could switch from his scheduled 1000m race to the Dream Mile. The IAAF, however, pressurised Norwegian promoter Arne Haukvik to keep him out of the race as they wanted Ovett and Coe to line up in their own Golden Mile race later in the season. 'We would have been thrilled to have Seb and Steve race each other in our stadium because it's the one the whole world wants to see,' remarked Haukvik. 'But we couldn't afford to upset the IAAF.'

So, the quibbling of athletics authorities became another factor in the drive to see Ovett and Coe together on a starting line. Coe therefore had to settle for the 1000m in which he set a new world record of 2:12.18. But even without him, the mile turned out to be widely acknowledged as the most thrilling four-lap race of all time. Ovett won convincingly in the third fastest recorded mile time — 3:49.25. He seemed content to merely fend off the challenge of the other runners (seven men ran faster than 3:51) when the record looked set to fall. 'It was a super race — one of the greatest I have ever been in,' said Ovett. Fourth-placed John Walker went further: 'That has to be the greatest mile race of all. At my age I should know. I seem to have run in most of them.'

Pacemaking and world record attempts had become the main features of the 1981 athletics season. For one reason or another, Ovett and Coe didn't meet in spiked combat and the alternative was running against each other's times. The IAAF, who prevented their Oslo clash, expressed their dislike of pacemaking by writing to national associations to ensure that all pacemakers finished races.

Ovett himself said after his Dream Mile victory, 'I think it was more important to win ... perhaps we're becoming a little too record conscious.' Coe was in agreement. 'It's time we started relying on our own judgement rather than complicated arrangements with pacemakers. The time has come when we should go out and do it alone.'

The most logical course of action would have been for them to go out and do it together, but it was not to be so. 'They won't run against each other because at the moment they're both number one,' said Steve Cram. 'And if they ran against each other, one of them would lose out. So it's all about chasing records. And to have world records these days you've got to have pacemakers. The summer of 1981 showed that world records are what the public want, so I can see no harm in it. Ovett and Coe certainly aren't capable of running these times on their own.'

The record-breaking attempts continued with Ovett dipping under 3 minutes 50 seconds in a mile race for the fourth time; no-one else had managed more than one. His time of 3:49.66 meant that he now had 4 of the 6 fastest mile times ever run to his credit. It seemed that the world record syndrome would be cleared by an Ovett–Coe clash in the Golden Mile, but the AAA were keen for the confrontation to take place on home soil, with the financial advantages going to the benefit of British athletics, and they pressurised Ovett to withdraw.

So it was back to dashing to beat the digits and a mere 21/100ths of a second separated Ovett from breaking his 1500m record in Budapest. Bob Benn and John Walker set the ideal pace but Ovett once again missed the record by delaying his finishing burst. After the race Ovett blamed himself, 'Everything was perfect. It was my mistake. I should have gone at the bell.' Nevertheless, Ovett's comfortable win, in 3:31.57, was the second fastest 1500m of all time; he could now claim to have recorded five of the nine quickest 1500m times ever run — as well as four of the six best miles.

Ovett's record stood for itself but Coe stole his thunder in Zurich in August. He had been aiming to run 3:46 for the mile (Ovett held the record at 3:48.8) and to better Ovett's 1500m record on the way. After missing the metric mile time, Coe went on to set a new mile record of 3:48.53.

Ovett jetted out to Berlin, intending to reclaim the record and announcing that he had finally severed his strong home ties. In a *Daily Mirror* article he revealed that his mother and father had refused to speak to him when he moved in with Rachel eleven months earlier; he later told reporters they would be marrying in September. In front of 22,000 spectators in Berlin's Olympic Stadium, Allan Wells showed that he was undisputedly the world's number one sprinter by winning the Golden Sprints title, but Ovett's winning mile time of 3:55.59 was well outside Coe's record.

Four days later, Ovett moved on to Koblenz's Oberwerth Stadium. Controversy marred the pre-race activities as Thomas Wessinghage led several runners who refused to run against Ovett in the mile because the 1500m had been the original distance scheduled in the meeting programme. Both events were therefore fitted into the meeting. And Steve Scott stole the limelight by clocking 3:31.95, the third ever fastest over 1500m.

Immediately after Scott finished, officials rushed forward with tape measures and chalk to calculate the correct starting point for the mile — a distance never previously run in Koblenz. Bob Benn set the perfect early pace: 55.63 seconds at 400m and 1:53.59 at 800m. James Robinson took Ovett to the bell and this time he had no hesitation in striking for home. Leaving a world class field floundering in his wake, he hit the tape 6 seconds clear of Craig Masback in a new world record of 3:48.40 — 0.13 seconds faster than Coe's Zurich time.

'I felt good all the way,' said Ovett. 'For once it wasn't raining or blowing, the conditions were perfect. When Robinson faded at the end of the third lap I wasn't worried.

I knew I had the record. I'm sure it could go even lower if everything is right on the night.'

Two days later everything was right on the night for Coe in his third attempt to break the mile record. In the Golden Mile, the Sheffield man brought an incredible climax to a record-crazy track season in lowering the record for the third time by clocking 3:47.33 ahead of Boit, Walker, Scott and Wessinghage. He had taken 1.07 seconds off Ovett's time. Middle distance running history had been turned on its head in nine days of glory, in which time the much prized world mile record had been smashed three times. When Coe gestured towards the stand in Brussels, an uncharacteristically venomous expression was clearly set on his face. He clearly felt he had scored a victory over the absent Ovett.

An editorial comment in *The Observer*, however, summed up the feelings of the impatient world at the latest astonishing developments in the rivalry between Coe and Ovett: 'There will be no complete satisfaction for them or us until they meet in the same race. Times, on their own, will join those other sporting statistics, like footballers' wages, that become too bewildering to mean anything. The races themselves will seem like the latest moves in a game of postal chess. If the true essence of the sport is to be served, the digital clocks must one day be put to one side, the pacemakers relieved of their painful sacrifice and the two must run against each other.'

As the season drew to a close, speculation about possible clashes on British soil in 1982 was in the air, but nothing tangible had been arranged to satisfy the punters. Nevertheless, Coe's recapturing the world mile record, allied to the astonishing new record he set for the 800m at the start of the season, meant that he had taken over in the driving seat.

But the season wasn't over yet. Ovett claimed a season's best time of 1:46.40 to win the 800m race at Crystal Palace's Amoco Games. He did just enough to hold off the challenge of Carlisle's 19-year-old Chris McGeorge, destined to be Britain's next great 800m runner. Then it was on to Rome, scene of his first major international breakthrough seven years earlier, as the 1981 season reached its climax in the shape of the World Cup.

Americanised South African Sydney Maree, who had been a pawn in mixed-up sporting political battles all summer, and Kenya's Mike Boit failed in their combined attempt to nullify the effect of Ovett's sprint finish; the Brighton runner winning comfortably in a time of 3:34.95. However, it wasn't the last he was to see of Maree.

After flying home to help Rachel with their wedding preparations, he returned to Rome two days later — arriving tired and dishevelled in the early hours of the morning — to run a mile race in Reiti, 70 north of the Italian capital. He may have expected a not too taxing end-of-the-season outing, but the race bore out Ovett's long-standing belief that his and Coe's almost total domination of the world middle distance stage would be broken sooner or later.

Ovett had taken Bob Benn along with him in the hope of beating Coe's mile record but tiredness overtook him in the home straight and Sydney ('The Shadow') Maree celebrated his 25th birthday by rocketing to the tape to inflict Ovett's first defeat in the mile for five years. Maree's time, 3:48.83, was the third fastest ever; nobody had run so fast without breaking the record. 'The runners were very tired,' said Ovett. 'There was only one man in the race who was ready and that was Maree.'

Thus the unfamiliar name of the Pretoria-born, Villanova University graduate broke the Ovett–Coe stranglehold. Many felt that the result might have been a fluke, but Maree gave further evidence that he will be a big threat to Ovett and Coe in the future when he missed breaking Ovett's 1500m record by less than a second (3:32.30 against Ovett's 3:31.36) in Hamburg the following week. After adding a 3:49.93 mile time to his credit, Maree wound up his season in style by winning New York's inaugural Fifth Avenue Mile in a storming time of 3:47.52.

Ovett, meanwhile, ended his season with a two mile victory in the IAC/Coca Cola meeting at Crystal Palace and three successful races in Australia, notably an 800m victory in the Commonwealth Games Preview Meeting in Brisbane.

The 1981 season had contained many milestones for Steve Ovett, but the most significant took place at Hove Registry Office on 18th September. Steve had met Rachel Waller seven years earlier when she was running at Crystal Palace; before she became a restaurant worker and model, Rachel was a county class hurdler with Medway AC. Sharing a keen interest in art with Steve, 23-year-old Rachel — a tall shapely brunette — set up home with Steve in Varndean Drive (which the *Brighton Argus* referred to as the 'Ovett love nest'), opposite his former school, following the Moscow Olympics.

It remains to be seen how Steve's marriage will affect his future — both on the track and off it. But one change is already assured. As Steve told friends before the wedding, 'I'll have to change the ILY signal to "I'll be home soon. Get the kettle on."'

'At the moment athletics is firmly in second place', said Steve after he and Rachel had put pen to paper. Wearing a smart, blue pin-stripe suit with a white rose in the lapel, a silver-grey tie and a broad smile, Ovett whisked his beautiful bride off to Kent for a two day honeymoon and then on to Australia, Hong Kong, Bali and Tasmania. To complete his day, Ovett's mother and father attended his wedding to reunite their strong ties.

As Steve settled into a new life in his and Rachel's seafront apartment in an elegant Hove crescent, he could reflect on a post Olympic run of events which completed the first chapter of his life culminating in the award of the MBE in the New Year's Honours List.

Seven

'Don't Follow Me, I'm Lost'

Few modern day sportsmen have cultivated a public image quite as intriguing, seemingly confused, yet distinctive as Steve Ovett. His long-standing battle with the British Press resulted in him adopting a tight-lipped stance, an almost unprecedented feature of our so called 'media age'. Most people's picture of Steve Ovett has therefore been the brusque, selfish, ruthless and arrogant one, painted by the popular Press. Ovett would be the first to admit that all of the above adjectives have sometimes been accurate, but the most intriguing feature of Steve Ovett is that this image hides the stronger side of his character. Beneath the hard and bland exterior is a gentle, compassionate, insecure and basically shy man.

The disguising of this nature stems back to 1975 and the argument in the Crystal Palace press-box, in which Ovett said he would probably not be running in the European Cup final as he planned to hitch-hike to Athens that weekend. 'Surely you can't be serious?' exclaimed at least one reporter. 'Where's your sense of patriotism?' Ovett stormed out leaving the Press to interview an empty chair.

Not since the flamboyant figure of David Bedford had the British athletics Press been faced with such a controversial character. And they responded by filling the following day's back pages with the stories of the unpatriotic, immature and arrogant young runner from Brighton. Ovett has given only a select number of interviews since that day and the situation was aggravated by the emergence of Sebastian Coe. His open and clean image was exactly what the Press needed to contrast Ovett and thus the great rivalry between the two was portrayed as an archetypal battle between Mr Nice Guy and Mr Nasty.

The confrontation between Ovett and Coe in Moscow prompted innumerable examples illustrating the Press's contrasting attitudes towards them. This was especially so following Coe's 1500m victory when the national newspapers were filled with such comments as: 'the gentleman proved that nice guys can win … he turned the tables on the brash young runner from Brighton …'; 'nice guys do win gold medals …'; 'it was immensely satisfying proof that nice guys are not ultimately condemned to failure …'; 'Seb is everyone's favourite, the nice guy we all wanted to win …'; 'Coe did more than win the gold medal yesterday. He lifted his soul, he enobled his art, he dignified his country …' and so on. 'Niceness' and 'nastiness', once only used in the domain of children's literature, had become an integral feature of British sports journalism.

Some of the Press have taken their dislike of Ovett to greater lengths. One leading sportswriter suggested that Ovett was 'perverse' to run against and beat Coe in the 1978 European Championships 800m Final. Following his world mile record run in Oslo in 1980, one reporter remarked about Ovett: 'The strange behaviour of this 24-year-old running recluse doesn't anger people any more. It baffles them. And yet his attitude somehow reflects the climate of international athletics. It may not yet be a world of shady wheelings and dealings involving sinister characters, but it's not far off.' The Press's view of Ovett is no different abroad. One Helsinki newspaper called him 'harder than stone like Graham Greene's Pinky in *Brighton Rock*'.

Originally, Ovett had no wish to balance his public image engendered by such comments. 'Who am I to criticise the Press?' he exclaimed in an *Athletics Weekly* interview. 'They obviously know more about athletics than me. As for the public, I'm not really bothered by what people think. If they want to see me as an arrogant bastard, good luck to them. I know what I feel and I know what the people I respect feel. That's important.'

In the same interview, Ovett went on to describe to Dave Cocksedge the reasons why he originally adopted his 'no interviews' policy: 'Two reasons. I got fed up with the British Press. They have this lazy, imperious attitude towards the athletes. We run our guts out on the track and if we've pleased them enough for them to want to talk to us we get this demand to attend the press-box interview room, like some sort of Royal Command. Then we have to sit there like good little boys and say what they expect us to say. But if we don't say what they expect us to say, or if we offend their sense of patriotism, we get branded as arrogant, immature upstarts, or there's something terribly wrong with us.'

'I got the impression in 75 that, because I wasn't talking as they'd programmed me to talk, they'd be better off interviewing an empty chair and inventing their own answers. That way they'd get the story they wanted, and everyone would he happy. I'm a person who speaks his mind and I'm not politically ambitious, so really the Press have no use for me. Because I'm not planning to sit on sports councils or governing bodies I don't have to cultivate the Press and be a darling little boy for them. It seems that the Press are only interested in people who speak their minds the way the Press wants them to.'

While Ovett may be accused of over-reacting, a trait which many of his friends recognise as a common feature in him, his other reason for severing all formal links with the Press indicates that he knew what he was doing. 'I didn't want to get caught up in the "gold medal fever" which sweeps British athletics every Olympic year,' he said. 'If you win a bit before the Games, the Press start labelling you a medal prospect, and very quickly the pressure builds up into more than you can handle.'

Ovett was talking specifically about the Montreal Olympics, in which the absence of pressure helped him very little, but one suspects that the pressure built up by the media prior to the Moscow Olympics must have played a vital role in deciding the outcome of Ovett's first clash with Coe — in the 800 metre final. Coe and his father are even to this day mystified by his loss of form, but perhaps the pressure of the pre-Games build up in which he played such a prominent role weighed too heavily on his shoulders and helped to blunt his natural racing edge.

Ranked as the outsider to gain the gold medal, Ovett certainly had sufficient incentive to employ his killer instinct to devastating effect. Although it would be the bane of any philosopher's life even to attempt to rationalise the Ovett–Coe situation in Moscow, the result of the 1500m backs up this story. Once Coe was 'dead and buried' in the media's eyes and the pressure transferred to Ovett, his sharp racing instinct returned. In many respects, the emergence of Coe as the 'good guy everybody wants to see win' was the perfect foil for Ovett to get on with his running with the minimum of pressure; and both men agree that pressure was the main factor in their races in the Russian capital.

While Ovett's attitude to the media undoubtedly helped him, one can also argue that he stretched it a little too far. The credibility of his silent stance was severely strained when he gave a series of three exclusive interviews to the *Sunday People* during the Moscow Olympics. This was a bitter pill for the rest of the Press to swallow, especially after Ovett had refused to receive a nomination as Sportsman of the Year from the Sportswriter's Association. Even then, it was his mother who turned it down on his behalf saying, 'Steven and his family cannot see how he can accept an award considering the coverage he has received from the athletic writers of the Press.'

Ovett certainly appeared to simultaneously shrug off and nurture his bad guy image. And, although he claims to be indifferent to his treatment at the hands of the Press, Ovett appeared to be tired of it when he spoke to Mel Watman in a 1979 *Athletics Weekly* interview. 'I've reached this sort of Howard Hughes syndrome, where not talking to the Press is doing more damage than talking to them,' he said. 'I take the Press with a pinch of salt. How can they possibly know what's good for me and what I do wrong? But I'm trying to change this image the Press seem to be trying to perpetuate. I wouldn't like to think that kids will think "that's the attitude to have" because it's false. This sort of "kick 'em in the backside and be objectionable all the time" attitude — that's not me.'

So, who is the real Steve Ovett? 'I don't think you'll ever find out,' says Ovett's friend Peter Francis. 'I doubt whether even Steve himself knows.' Such an assertion only hardens the resolve to dig deeper and the more you dig the more it becomes apparent that, even to his friends, Steve Ovett appears to possess two or three personalities rolled up into one mass of contrast and contradiction.

Like an actor, Ovett can draw on different characters to suit changing circumstances. As Matt Bruce, his former art master says, 'You only have to look at Steve's face for a couple of minutes to see the quintessence of his character. His facial expressions portray so many different people and it can change in a flash — from the sparkling expressive-eyed man with the wide, engaging grin, to the aloof, expressionless boy, who's a million miles away.'

Despite his variable character, Ovett retains at least one constant feature. Says Bruce, 'In a very quiet and unassertive way, you could always feel Steve's presence. It was never imposing. He doesn't draw attention upon himself by being noisy or anything. But his quiet, unassuming charm stood him apart from everyone else. He just draws you towards himself. Another prominent characteristic was that he could never be positive until he had a pair of spikes on his feet.'

People who knew Ovett well in his formative years and as a teenager will, to a man, tell you that he was 'basically shy and insecure'. Reg Hook, the President of Brighton and Hove Athletic Club who has known Steve since he was a 10-year-old, says, 'He's most uncomfortable in the company of adults and I think he has always found it difficult to make relationships. You're never sure he's listening to anything you're saying, let alone taking it in. He'll answer you sometimes, but he never appears to be *there*!'

Ovett's first coach Barry Tilbury agrees. 'He's always been shy and never a person you could have a deep or meaningful conversation with. He tends to talk in clichés and will throw in the odd give-away line and then jog off. No commitment. You won't get an opinion out of him and he won't stand and talk to you.'

Cliff Temple (athletics correspondent for *The Sunday Times*) says he has 'always found Steve's conversation stimulating when we're alone, in front of a tape-recorder'. But he adds, 'Sometimes when you approach Steve he naturally backs away and you find yourself walking backwards for 100 yards or so while trying to hold a conversation. He likes to feel able to walk free if necessary. He will throw in a punch-line and go— he's a bit like the Royals in that respect, not wishing to get involved in a conversation. In company, he can change from being the life and soul of the party with an answer for everything, into a withdrawn introvert, content to gaze, preoccupied, into space.'

Dave Cocksedge, a journalist who was very close to Steve between 1970 and 1979 says, 'One day Steve can be friendly, another day he'll stand next to you and won't say a word for half an hour. Basically, I think he is shy.' This is the Steve Ovett the general public don't know, the one he hides behind a barrier of indifference. They are only aware of the seemingly arrogant runner with the killer instinct, but even that Steve Ovett is not the *real* one.

Says Reg Hook, 'Steve takes the attitude that whatever happens on the running track is in no way connected with Steve Ovett the person. He thinks that the person you see on the track is completely different. He's genuinely disturbed by the attention his running receives and that's why he can be brusque.' Ovett himself has said, 'I enjoy being myself 90% of the time and Steve Ovett the runner just 10% of the time.'

Far from indicating any traces of madness, this unique form of schizophrenia is probably the ideal foil for the many and varied pressures which accompany modern day sporting superstardom. 'I don't think I'm mad,' said Ovett in a 1978 interview with Cliff Temple. 'But sometimes I just don't seem to bother about things that are the most important in my life. The World Cup race in Dusseldorf should have been life or death for me. Yet it didn't feel like that at all. It was as though I was completely detached from what was happening and yet taking an active part. It's a contradiction in me that I don't even know what I'm doing myself.'

This image of Ovett as a confused genius was very prominent between 1977 and early 1979, when he was unquestionably the world's number one middle distance runner. It followed what many could call his arrogant phase, but since the rise of Sebastian Coe it has become increasingly obvious that Steve Ovett has matured into a man with a clear sense of perspective. For example, he told Patrick Collins in the *Evening News* that his once all-consuming desire to win an Olympic gold medal had waned: 'Why should I invest my whole life in a race that happens one afternoon every four years? I go round Brighton some days and see people, young people, who'd give anything to walk, much less run. And here I am in perfect health surrounded by a marvellous family. I mean, that's really important, isn't it? — I hope I haven't given you the impression that I don't enjoy the sport. It's because I love it so much that I want to get it in its right perspective.'

So, if this man who spent his days pounding the streets of Brighton and Hove, wasn't motivated by the lure of Olympic gold, what kept him going? 'I've thought about it a lot and I can't find any answer,' Ovett told Temple in *The Sunday Times*. 'Except that I enjoy discovering myself through running. That's why, when I try to explain it to anyone who is achievement orientated, they can't understand me — because there is no specific goal. There is no path I follow. I feel as if I'm just drifting along, because although I can progress physically through my training, mentally and spiritually I don't know what the hell I'm doing. It's like that car sticker: "Don't follow me, I'm lost".'

And he told Mel Watman in *Athletics Weekly*: 'I can't understand myself. I don't know how I'm going to end up, and although I should be I'm not really bothered. At least I've enjoyed myself from my start in athletics to when I'm finished. Many people work in jobs they don't like doing from the time they leave school to when they die.

'For me, it's more than enough to enjoy things day to day ... I'm just meandering through life and appreciating what I can when I can. I enjoy home life, I enjoy running, I enjoy doing things other people can't do because they haven't got the time. Eventually I'll have to change. I can't go on living with my parents for ever, but for the moment I'm quite happy. I'm just a child, I suppose, really!'

Shortly after this interview, Ovett's life did begin to change and two principal factors drew him out of that prolonged 'childhood'. The first was his relationship with young model Rachel Waller, with whom he became deeply involved. She led him away from his rather sheltered life with his parents in Harrington Villas. The second factor was Sebastian Coe's world record breaking spree in the summer of 1979.

Says Cliff Temple: 'Steve had too much time on his hands when he was at home and the fact that Coe suddenly leap-frogged over him to the top spot in world middle distance running preyed heavily on his mind. The first thing it did was to contradict his comments a few months earlier that going for world records was "senseless". That showed that this mysterious character was human after all. If he'd resisted the temptation of chasing records he would have perpetuated this air of mystique he had built up for much longer.

'The emergence of Coe also made him look at himself. He changed from this confused "don't follow me" character into a much more relaxed person with clearer objectives. It brought him out of his shell. Before he left home I think he led a very sheltered life and his character became even more complete when he went out into the world on his own at the end of 1980. John Walker and many other athletes have remarked to me that Steve seems a lot more mature these days.'

Nevertheless, the influence of Steve's parents had a marked influence on his life. In particular they provided him with an ideal situation in which he could develop into a world class athlete without having to worry about various external pressures. And they gave him what he valued most — his independence. 'I'm not obliged to anybody,' he told Mel Watman in 1979. 'I haven't got a boss who can come up to me and say "why didn't you run for your country?" I haven't accepted sponsorship, so sponsors can't say "this is bad publicity". The British Amateur Athletic Board and the Sports Aid Foundation don't give me money, so I don't have to answer to them ... this may upset some people but that's the advantage I've got — I'm not that obliged!'

The pressures of international athletics have increasingly repulsed Ovett the closer he moved to the top of the athletics tree. 'I'm not obsessed by athletics,' he said in *Athletics Weekly*. 'If someone said to me tomorrow "you're going to have to stop world athletics" I wouldn't throw myself off Beachy Head. If I'm running well then great, I enjoy it, that's what the sport is there for. It's not for putting yourself under intense pressure all the time, feeling sick all the time, coming home and being depressed, and all that. Good grief!'

Since the day Steve Ovett won every race at school by the proverbial street or two, he has had to live with the pressure of being expected to win in every race — even the English Cross Country Championships. So many things can go wrong to prevent such a victory happening and if he loses it is a major shock, yet if he does win there is no surprise. Part of the enjoyment of victory is the shock result — like Sunderland's 1973 FA Cup win or Ovett's Olympic

800m triumph and Coe's subsequent win in the 1500m. Being confidently expected to win in most races, Ovett has rarely been in a position to savour the 'other half' of triumph. He has never been the under-dog, dreaming of the day when people would finally acclaim him, which is the motivation which drives on so many athletes.

To those of us — particularly journalists — who find it difficult to identify with the kind of pressure involved in being an Olympic favourite, Ovett gave an ideal empathy analogy when he told Mel Watman in *Athletics Weekly*: 'Suppose I was to say to you: next year on such and such a date you're going to write an article in fifteen minutes and it's going to be the best article of your life, and not only that but there's going to be eight other correspondents writing the same thing and we're going to select the best ... and if you don't get selected, that's it, your life is a failure.

'It's a bit hard, isn't it? The public and media put us under that stress and I think it's rather a false situation to get into. Everyone thinks that anyone who gets an Olympic gold medal is something different, something mystical — which is not true. I know a lot of complete idiots who are Olympic champions and I know a lot of great athletes who never were. I think as long as you enjoy your running and enjoy life then Olympic golds and things like that are secondary really.'

This desire to diffuse as much pressure as possible has helped Ovett to perpetuate a withdrawn, Garbo-like image, which many of his friends claim he enjoyed. But his reasons for doing so were not particularly born out of excessive self-indulgence or an aversion to awkwardness. As he explained to Mel Watman, 'I'm not wrapped up in athletics. I think a lot of so-called athletes are now paying the price of fabricating images through various PR situations and through the media. Staying away from sponsors, television and the Press to a certain extent really lessens the fabrication of Steve Ovett Superstar and enhances my chances of running better on the track.' And in an ITV interview, he commented, 'It's a matter of self-protection. I don't want to become public property.'

On the running track, however, Ovett can allow himself to become public property for a few minutes as the extrovert side of his nature takes over. His fetish for waving to the crowd as he swoops past his floundering opponents off the final bend has lost Ovett a lot of friends, especially among the athletics fraternity. But Ovett claims, 'There's no malice towards other competitors and I don't think there's any arrogance there at all. I cannot see why other people get so upset about it. I just do it because I'm excited. I mean I'm not the archetypal Englishman who wipes his brow, put his tracksuit on and walks back to a cup of tea!'

The crowds pack into stadia all over the world to witness his track antics and there can be little doubt that the Crystal Palace crowd, in particular, love every minute of it. 'I suppose they like to see me wave and I enjoy doing it; it works both ways,' he told Mel Watman. 'At the Coca Cola meeting (in 1978) ... when I stepped out on to the track the whole of the back straight just stood up and applauded. It overwhelmed me; I didn't know what to do.'

Like Brendan Foster and David Bedford before him, Ovett has become a King of the Crystal Palace crowd, the home of British athletics, which is itself a supreme accolade. 'There is that kind of rapport, which seems strange to me, because I'm probably the first athlete who hasn't given a lot of time to image projection. I don't appear on TV and I don't say the right things at the right time like a lot of other athletes, yet despite that and a lot of bad press coverage the crowd are still with me. And the people showed, particularly with the BBC Sports Personality Award, that they are still for me and I think that's fabulous.'

Intentionally or not, Ovett has certainly projected a distinctive image. It is part of the crowd's attraction to him and it has helped him to surround himself with an aura of invincibility, which puts his fellow competitors at a disadvantage often before they have even set foot on the track. His first coach Barry Tilbury says, 'Even at an early age he had this air that he could always cope with anything. He always looked very easy doing work others struggled with and he appeared quite capable of stepping up a further gear if necessary.

'There has always been a touch of the Muhammad Ali about him. In certain cases I'm sure he's deliberately gone out of his way to cultivate this mysterious/showman side of his nature by doing stupid things like running half-marathons in the middle of the track season. Nobody else, not even Coe, would dare do that — let alone stand a chance of succeeding at it. He's created such an air of invincibility that his opponents don't even think about beating him, which is half his battle won. Forget about the records and the medals. To get yourself in that kind of situation is really something else — especially in such a raw competitive sport as running.'

This could be an example of Ovett's apparently arrogant or impetuous actions appearing to be more like the actions of a shrewd young man. True to the Swedish meaning of his name, Steve Ovett is something of a wisen owl underneath the Borg-like invincible exterior. Says Ovett (in *Athletics Weekly*), 'I have a rather casual approach really, but I suppose this image has been lost with this sort of ruthless, cold-hearted James Dean image that the Press seem to give me. People think "don't talk to him, he'll bite your head off" or "he knows what he's doing, he'll be ready". It's not me. I panic the same as everybody else.'

Ovett gave a fascinating insight into the real Steve Ovett in an excellent interview with Patrick Collins in the *Evening News* in 1978 — 'Sometimes I almost despair. I mean all I'm really after is the simple life. I've got a smashing family who I enjoy being with and I've got a marvellous sport I enjoy taking part in. That's it. Full stop. I'm a very uncomplicated sort of fellow. But if you're a sportsman in Britain, people won't leave it at that. They want to own a bit of you. "Why don't you give more interviews, Steve? What's your opinion on this issue, Steve? ... Why didn't you run that race a bit faster? ...

Don't you care about your image, Steve?"

'Well the truth is I don't really care about my image because I don't think I'm doing anything that's terribly important. Sure, I immerse myself in athletics, but I won't let myself drown. It doesn't obsess me. If I had to pack it all in tomorrow, I'd be sad, but not suicidal. It's the people who would become suicidal who're the ones with something to worry about. It disturbs me the way a lot of athletes overestimate themselves these days. The media are always convinced that they're very important people. I think they resent me for not wanting to be part of that.

'A woman from "Superstars" rang me once to ask which week I'd appear. I said "Never" and she was shocked — "I can't accept that," she said, "what would my producer say?" They think you're going to leap at them because you're a sportsman and you don't know any better. Even in your own sport you're not really free ... you're told where to run. They don't exactly tell you they've got telly contracts in mind, but that's what they mean.

'If I'd won the 800m at the Montreal Olympics, I'd have walked straight out of international athletics. No question. I'd talked with my family about it and my mind was made up. As it happened it didn't arise because Juantorena came from nowhere and made the event a bloody bore by being so brilliant. But if I'd got the gold, that was me finished.

'You see, people would have been queuing up to knock me down. Any failure after that wouldn't have been tolerated. I'd have been public property, and I couldn't have stood that. It happened to Brendan Foster after Montreal. He doesn't run in races he thinks he might lose these days, therefore he misses out on races which would benefit his ultimate planning. I'd have done the same thing. The more frightened of defeat you become, the more the pressure piles on. I don't need that.'

Having entered that position, Ovett would seem to be contradicting himself by carrying on when he stands to lose everything. But he still has another peak to aim at in the shape of Sebastian Coe. And his love of running would also be difficult to overcome — 'You find out a lot about yourself through athletics. If you're cut out to be a winner or a failure or a quitter, athletics will bring it out of you, You're always stripping yourself down to the bones of your personality. And sometimes you just get a glimpse of the kind of talent you've been given. Sometimes I run and I don't even feel the effort of running. I don't even feel the ground. I'm just drifting. Incredible feeling. All the agony and frustration, they're all justified by one moment like that'.

Ovett's claim that he is not drowning in athletics is true. He is a gifted sculptor and photographer and has commented, 'I love painting and use that to stretch my mind and find out more about myself.' Ovett is also a keen reader and angler and his artist bent is complemented by a mechanical brain. He enjoys nothing better than an afternoon spent messing about with a car engine. He owns a Range Rover and a Jaguar XJS which boasts the personalised number plate SJO 20 (this eccentricity is even echoed on his running spikes, which have the 'Nike' brand name blanked out on the heel tabs and superimposed with 'Ovett').

Nevertheless, Ovett's day revolves around athletics; everything else being of secondary importance. His training partner Matt Paterson knocks him up at 7.30 every morning for a five to eight mile run, during which they will discuss any topic under the sun except running. 'Sometimes we have sleet lashing straight down in our faces and our hands are numb,' says Ovett. 'All around us people are rushing off to work. It's times like that I feel there must be an easier way of life.' Yet — as the late James Coote pointed out — 'to miss just one run could mean the difference between success and failure in a sport where achievements are measured in 1/100ths of seconds.'

After showering and breakfasting, Steve usually slips back into bed and sleeps until noon. He then runs a solo ten miles on the South Downs, after which relaxation in the afternoon is of prime importance. He will fill in time by listening to his extensive record collection, wandering along the seafront to the shops, tinkering with an engine or by going back to bed. When Paterson returns from school in the evening, the two men go for a five mile fartlek session in nearby woods.

'People who think I have a glamorous lifestyle should try it sometimes,' Ovett commented to Dave Cocksedge in *Jogging*. 'It requires a lot of self-discipline and it's often a grind. They call it dedication. I often get depressed with it all when it's just not going well, but I still get up and get out there for a run. It's a fact of life — like hitting your head against a brick wall. You just keep going. I often think I've had enough of the sport and the people in it and I want to get away, but I always come back and get on with my training in the end.'

'I just love running fartlek in the woods,' he said in *Athletics Weekly*. 'I can't stand running in circles on the track; that doesn't appeal to me. Maybe I could perform a lot better if I did a bit of track training, but I don't think so. I made the mistake before Montreal of being too obsessed with tracks and the stopwatch — it just wasn't me. I love running over the Downs and I'll be running over them when I'm finished with top class athletics. It's just what relaxes me.'

Another notable feature of Steve Ovett's character is his keen wit. The teenage international athlete adept at predicting the length of after-dinner speeches turned into the young man who would display his tongue-in-cheek humour in the letters column of *Athletics Weekly,* such as the following:

'Dear Sir,

Correction: Steve Ovett's 200m time earlier this season (1975) was 21.7 not 22.7.

After being told the official time at the end of the race, there was no more sceptical person than myself. So I queried it. 'Your time is 21.7'. Again I queried the time. 'Your time is 21.7!'

So you see my time is 21.7 and what you or anyone else says

two months later doesn't mean a thing to me, as I fail to see how seconds can be added to people's time after the event has happened.

If this is normal practice, however, then I shall have to run most of my races earlier in the season next year, in order to give you more time to adjust them.'

Present day Ovett humour includes such antics as wearing a horned 'devil' cap in front of the Crystal Palace press-box. And if you ring Steve's home the voice you're most likely to hear is that of Vincent Price. 'My dear, your words are falling on deaf ears,' proclaims the master of suspense, in the tones he usually reserves for renditions of Edgar Alan Poe's most chilling tales. 'The person you want is all tied up now,' continues the recorded message. 'If you care to leave a message, just wait for the signal and whatever you say will be recorded for eternity.'

Despite his many rows and controversies, Ovett has always been warmly regarded by one particular section of the community. He never tires of the company of children and they hero worship him, almost without exception. He once said, 'I love kids and would do anything to help them.' For many years the over-riding passion in his spare time has been his involvement with the handicapped children of Sussex. And despite his aversion to publicity a number of his activities have been chronicled.

Whenever he crosses the finishing line at Crystal Palace, instead of ascending the steps to the Press interview room Ovett will make straight for the 'disabled pen' and spend sometimes hours signing autographs and chatting to the wheelchair-bound spectators. 'I sometimes think about all those people who are ill or crippled and would give anything to walk, let alone run,' he told Dave Cocksedge in *Jogging*. 'Then I realise just how lucky I am. When the training becomes a struggle, I often think of that, and it can humble you.'

Money-raising fun-runs, church services, hospital visits and the like are all an integral part of Ovett's week. He turns down invitations to all kinds of functions by the score, saying, 'I don't want to be public property,' but if the event involves young people his acceptance of the invitation is almost automatic. When readers of the *Brighton Argus* voted him their 'Sportsman of the Year' in 1978 it was said that apart from his athletic achievements what clinched the vote was his 'willingness to mix with and help young local athletes'.

It was during that memorable year that Steve made a rare appearance in a razzamatazz charity fund-raising event. He agreed to play in a team alongside his father and other Brighton market traders in a charity cricket match against a Showbiz XI that raised more than £1,000 for the Variety Club of Great Britain. Far more typical of the invitations he accepts was his appearance as chief guest at a children's religious service at Brighton's St. Mathias Church. His presence resulted in the church's largest ever congregation. Hundreds of local youngsters handed over donations which amounted to £333 for the Church of England Children's Society.

When Steve returned to Brighton after the Moscow Olympics, he fended off moves for a civic reception and, while criticism mounted, plunged into a welter of activities to help the under-privileged, apologising for not having been able to fulfil all requests before Moscow. He responded to a plea from the staff of Brighton's Royal Alexandra Hospital for Sick Children to make a morale-boosting visit to see 10 year old spina bifida patient Graham Smith. A devoted fan of Steve's, Graham was awaiting a vital operation and surprise at seeing his hero at his bedside turned to astonished delight when Ovett handed over his Olympic gold and bronze medals to keep as good luck charms until after his operation.

Senior House Officer, Dr Alison Smith was appreciative of Steve's efforts, saying, 'Steve really made Graham's day. He's a very caring person and his kind gesture boosted Graham's morale tremendously. He was admitted during the Olympics and was anxious to watch all of Steve's races.' Ovett once again shunned publicity, but his sister Sue told reporters, 'He absolutely adores kids. He makes quite a few trips to see disabled children. It's something he does for his own pleasure as well as the children's but he rarely mentions them — not even to the family.'

Rachel, with whom Steve was now living, added further praise. 'A lot of people have got the idea that Steve is a stand-offish sort of person,' she said. 'But he likes to do these things and really cares for people, although he likes to do it in his own quiet way. He doesn't like to shout about it from the rooftops.' The mother of the little boy was so appreciative that she wrote the following letter to *Athletics Weekly*:

'Steve's own family had not even seen his medals when he gave them to Graham to look after for him and to show to the other children when he was better. He left as quietly as he had arrived after promising to wave in his race at Crystal Palace that evening and the medals were returned three weeks later. If there were a lot more Steve Ovetts the world would be a far nicer and happier place to live in.'

In fact Ovett's promise to wave to Graham gave his enemies the moment they had been waiting a long time for when Ireland's John Treacy pipped him on the line to win the 5,000m at the Coca Cola meeting. But Ovett's gesture was typical of the man who, a few years earlier, promptly gave a portable radio presented to him after a race victory to the nearest wheelchair-bound spectator he met.

Shortly afterwards, Steve delighted the staff of Chailey Heritage Craft School by joining in the wheelchair races at the East Sussex sports day for physically handicapped children. He spent a whole day competing inexpertly against the seven to sixteen-year-old pupils at Chailey, where rock star Ian Dury — who has also done so much to help the disabled — spent his youth as a victim of polio. 'He came across as a very warm and caring person,' said deputy headmistress Margaret Bruce. 'He was very genuine. If anyone comes and is patronising with the children they clam up and don't relate to them at all. But they so obviously enjoyed Steve's company and enjoyed him as a person.

person.

'Involvement with sport is very important to the youngsters. Too many people think that the handicapped should stay in wheelchairs but they are full of the same teenage exuberance as others and sport is an ideal outlet for them. Steve's visit was a really pleasant surprise. I'm sure the children felt a part of the big sports scene with someone like Steve to relate to. He was eager to get involved and was excellent with the kids.'

After spending a rare afternoon of losing every race he entered, Steve cemented his friendship with 150 competitors by patiently signing his autograph on everything pushed under his nose: an avalanche of books, magazines, T-shirts, and a score of plaster-casts. A year later, when the event was about to be re-staged, the organisers — who had received an advance promise from Steve of a return appearance — heard with disappointment the news that his marriage was set for the preceding week and their sports day was set to clash with his honeymoon. But their fears were banished when Steve told them, 'I made a promise to come nine months ago, and that date is still in my diary. I'll be there.' And he was.

As with his running, Steve Ovett's involvement with handicapped children has consumed him, but not to the point of turning him into a bland, pretentious crusader. It springs from a deep rooted human compassion which is as much an integral feature of Steve Ovett's character as his showmanship on the running track and his shyness off it. While helping to launch a Sussex County Guide for the Disabled in 1981, which listed public buildings, shops and hotels with easy access for the infirm, he said, 'I find it sad that we have to be reminded to take care of the disabled. It's something we should do all of the time.'

Respect for Ovett's charity work is widespread in athletic circles. TV commentator Ron Pickering — who coached Lynn Davies to a memorable Olympic long-jump victory in 1974 — has followed the Brighton runner's charity exploits with great interest ever since Ovett gave him his Olympic tracksuit to help a fund-raising venture at his club, Haringey AC. Ovett 'promoted' the article's sale with a personal appearance. 'There is not one British athlete who has ever given more to the handicapped than Steve Ovett,' says Ron. 'He is the sort of person who doesn't support charities at arm's length. He is involved with those kids, picking them up, carrying them and getting to know them.

'His concern is absolutely genuine. He just thinks that he's the luckiest guy alive to be able to run, and therefore those who aren't so lucky aught to be fostered and nurtured along. He does a marvellous job — far more than anyone else I know in sport. On that score alone, Steve deserves a better reputation. Plus the fact that he's a very nice, articulate person who happens to be very warm and very human.'

Steve Ovett's concern for others extends to his fellow competitors, not least of all the young athletes who will take his place one day at the top of the highly competitive British middle distance running fraternity. Carlisle athlete Chris McGeorge has — in the past three years — been the only British junior 800m runner to match the talent that young Steve Ovett showed at the same age. They met for the first time at the Amoco Games in 1981 when the aimiable nineteen-year-old Cumbrian pushed Ovett right to the tape. Afterwards, Ovett spent the best part of an hour passing on tips and advice to McGeorge.

'Steve told me that he thought we would have run against each other a lot earlier,' recalls Chris. 'He told me that, with a bit more strength and experience, it wouldn't be long before I started leaving him behind in the home straight. He struck me as a gentle and warm person. In comparison with Seb, the athletes would see him as the extrovert; Seb tends to be more subdued and with his father all of the time. The thing they have most in common, apart from their running talent, is the fact that they're both wonderful people. When Seb broke the world mile record in Zurich he sent me a message wishing me luck in the European

Junior Championships. I couldn't believe that he could be so considerate. It just shows that they are not immersed in their own lives. Underneath their contrasting public images, they're both very human.'

Steve Cram, who has accompanied Ovett on his record-breaking sojourn in Europe in the past two years, says of him: 'He's a very likeable bloke. Everyone involved with athletics will tell you how nice he is. He's very helpful to the other athletes. And he really enjoys his athletics — he didn't get involved to make a name for himself.'

In December 1976, the Belgian runner Ivo Van Damme was killed in a car crash in Southern France, less than six months after collecting two Olympic silver medals at the age of 22. The big, bearded, middle distance runner had hoped to break the world 800m record in 1977 and to win the European 1500m title the following year. But for the fatal and tragic accident there could be no doubt that we would today talk about Van Damme, Ovett and Coe in the same context. The sadness of his death had a double edge; the loss of a great athlete and the loss of a great man. The man who best summed up those two feelings of loss was Steve Ovettt, who wrote the following letter to *Athletics Weekly*:

> 'It was a terrible shock for me to hear of the tragic death of Ivo Van Damme. Athletes are a strange breed who tend to have a certain disrespect for fate, believing that it plays little or no part in their lives or those of their fellow athletes. Only when something of this nature happens are we all shaken, and we take it hard. To win two silver medals in any Olympics is a fabulous performance; to win them in only your first Games and at the age of 22 marks the greatness of the man who must surely have gone on to greater honours.
>
> 'I do not think the significance of the death of a friend or someone close is truly recognised immediately; it only comes with time and on odd occasions. As a friend I will miss him at the beginning of races when we used to worry and joke together, during then when we both raced hard, and then finally afterwards — the sharing of the joy and disappointment we both recognised in each other.

'Now all I feel is a certain numbness at the loss of a friend and the emptiness that will be left when it goes.

'My sympathy goes to his parents and friends.'

Steve Ovett values his privacy and prefers to keep his private life out of the limelight. At the core of his character is a shy man who genuinely feels unsettled by people clamouring for what he calls 'a bit of me' — whether that 'bit' may take the form of a magazine article, a public appearance or even this book. However, Joe Public was undoubtedly provided with a distorted image of one of the world's greatest ever sportsmen. It has only been since injury wrecked his 1982 season that Ovett himself decided to re-shape the image to its true form — a form which delineates a deep-thinking, perceptive and intelligent man who now appears to be anything but lost.

Eight

A Brand New Ovett

The events of late 1981 and 1982 have taken the Steve Ovett story to an intriguing juxtaposition.

For the best part of a decade, Steve Ovett the athlete had spiralled almost too easily towards sporting immortality. Since he shrugged aside the potentially devastating effects of glandular fever in early 1974, his yearly improvement had always been significant — and perhaps best underlined by his achievements during the 1981 track season, which had been gained from a nominal amount of background training.

At only 26, Ovett had won every possible honour: Olympic and European gold medals, world records — 'the lot'. Apart from proving once and for all that he was Coe's superior, there seemed little else for Ovett to achieve. Yet the story of Steve Ovett the athlete still appeared to be lacking a vital chapter.

To most people that chapter contained the story of his inevitable demise — almost all of the athletics figures I questioned about Ovett's future were convinced that he had passed his peak. Steve Cram, for example, said, 'There is only one way Steve can go now and that will bring him closer to the likes of myself, Steve Scott and Tom Wessinghage. The odds in the Ovett-Coe stakes are changing dramatically in favour of Seb. I think Steve is past his best, whereas Seb is still at his peak.'

The one dissenting opinion came from Reg Hook, the president of Brighton and Hove AC, Steve's former club. 'Steve's very cagey as an athlete and is often satisfied with knowing he could have run a better race if he wanted to,' said Reg. 'He's very conscious of the fact that he doesn't have to exert himself in most races. He has always done just enough to break a record but when he is really pushed we will really see what he is capable of doing. I don't think any race has managed to bring the best out of him yet.'

This was one of the most curious aspects of the Steve Ovett story up to the winter of 1981. He had achieved everything in athletics, even appeared to be past his best to most observers, yet his full potential remained untapped. Ovett even acknowledged this himself after equalling Coe's 1500m record in Oslo in 1980. 'It's unnerving to think I equalled the world record when I was only jogging for two laps ... I wasn't even trying,' he said. 'I'm such a lazy bastard that I could finish athletics without ever knowing my full potential.'

Significantly, many people believed that Ovett was at his peak during his magnificent 1980 season. Could it therefore be possible that because he had never been fully extended while at his peak, the best of Steve Ovett would never in fact be seen? The manner in which Ovett rose to that peak and then appeared to dilute the strength of his 1981 season by running too many high class races suggested that this might be happening — without Ovett realising it. His running career needed a jolt, and it received two or three in 1982 : two or three jolts which could ultimately help Ovett realise his full potential.

'I definitely ran too often in too many high quality races in 1981,' admitted Ovett in the *Sunday Mirror*. 'There wasn't an easy race for me throughout the year. At the same time, my personal life was going through a transition. I'd left home, set up on my own, had a wedding to plan ... it was a hectic year.' After his long and tiring season, he therefore took two months off training, during which time he concentrated on decorating his new flat. But it wasn't long before Ovett's name was once again back in the headlines.

The failure to settle the Ovett-Coe issue during the 1981 season had left a lot of athletics fans wondering whether a clash would ever take place. Where once there was anticipation among the general public about the burning sporting issue of the day now there was an air of indifference, apathy and scepticism. To most athletics buffs, however, Coe and Ovett's studied avoidance of one another had been deeply frustrating. American athletics writer Bob Hersh captured that mood of frustration in an article for *Track and Field News*.

'The recognised heroes of our sport have been the men and women who have been willing to test their skills against anyone who would dare challenge their status as "numero uno",' wrote Hersh. 'Ovett and Coe are both chicken-hearted; they are pussycats masquerading as tigers. They can both run very fast, but neither has the confidence that defines a true champion. One of these days, somebody will come along who has the ability to run faster than Coe or Ovett has ever run, and who will gladly demonstrate his prowess over both of them. Then the Britons' places in history will be well-established and it will be clear forever that Sebastian Coe was never a great champion and neither was Steve Ovett. They were fast but insecure men, possessed of far more talent than courage.'

Shortly after the publication of Hersh's article, it was announced that 'after mutual haggling' Ovett and Coe had agreed to race each other three times during the summer of 1982. The behind-the-scenes wheelings and dealings of Coe's agents, Mark McCormack's IMG, and AAA official Andy Norman — Ovett's close friend and racing advisor — had arranged a mutually lucrative deal which would see the two runners clashing over 3,000m (at Crystal Palace, on July 17th), 800m (at Nice, on 14th August) and the mile (at Eugene, Oregon, USA, on 25th September).

Ironically, the morning after the dramatic announcement, Ovett was lying on an operating table in London's West Middlesex hospital. Thirty-six hours of dramatic developments in the Ovett-Coe saga were completed by the news that Ovett had badly injured himself on the railings of a church near to his Hove flat.

While out on a training run, he had glanced up at details of a Carol Service on the church noticeboard and toppled over some protruding railings, thus puncturing a thigh muscle and badly tearing ligaments.

For several weeks the proposed series hung very much in the balance. Following an operation, Ovett's leg healed very slowly. The healing process was complicated when muscle wastage caused his right thigh to shrink by 1½ inches, something which was eventually cleared by a revolutionary muscle building machine. Ovett nevertheless gradually clawed his way back to fitness and was in sufficiently good shape to tackle his old 'friend' the Big Dipper on his annual Easter training trip to Merthyr Mawr.

After returning from Wales, Ovett concentrated on feathering his financial nest and completely re-vamping his media image. He surprisingly agreed to participate in a rather stiff press conference with Sebastian Coe to publicise their 3,000m clash at Crystal Palace, looking very much the more relaxed and natural of the two. This was followed with an appearance on the all-star edition of 'A Question of Sport' on FA Cup Final morning. Could this be the same Steve Ovett who once distained the 'Famous Person syndrome' and who was once repulsed by TV sporting razzmatazz?

Three days later, U Bix Copiers Ltd issued the following press release: 'U Bix are fast off the mark to become the first British company to sign Steve Ovett under a three year, £80,000 contract with the British Amateur Athletic Board. Under the terms of the agreement Ovett will appear on behalf of the company at specified sporting and promotional events through to the end of 1984. His commitment to U Bix will include personal appearances on a number of occasions, dealer network support and other associated sales incentive activities. He may also feature in U Bix press, radio and TV advertisements.'

Steve (he once of the Garbo image) Ovett was well and truly coming out of his self-constructed shell. He attended the U Bix Challenge Cup Meeting at Gateshead between England, Australia, Yugoslavia and Czechoslovakia on June 13th, but purely in a promotional capacity as he had developed a slight groin strain.

Watching from the stands, his main interest was undoubtedly in the 3,000m, a race won by Dave Moorcroft after Steve Cram had limped out of the action on the first lap. With British athletics fans still holding their breath in anticipation of the triple Ovett-Coe showdown, few could have anticipated to what extent the deeds of both Moorcroft and Cram would push Ovett and Coe into the background during the 1982 track season.

A week later Ovett unexpectedly lined up for his first race of the season in the Southern Counties Championships at Crystal Palace. Much to the astonishment of the 100 or so spectators and the other shadowed Paul Chester of Stevenage until 300m out before competitors in the 1500m heats, the Olympic champion coasting to victory in 3:47.25. It was almost 16 seconds down on his world record performance at the distance, but Ovett had run smoothly and well within himself and his time was faster than his opening run in three out of the previous five seasons.

'The race was a mental rather than physical barrier,' said Ovett, who afterwards withdrew from the final. 'It was all a problem of persuading oneself to start somewhere. I was leaving it longer and longer and on the Saturday morning, when I was doing a few strides with friends in Brighton, I suddenly realised that if I missed the Southerns I would end up in July without a single race behind me.'

With that testing run behind him, Ovett suddenly found himself pitched into the fray of the 1982 European circuit. Coe withdrew from the Bislett Games at Oslo on June 26th and Ovett stepped in to replace his arch rival as a "personal favour" to meeting promoter Sven Arne Hansen. Ovett clearly wasn't fit enough for such a high standard of competition and it came as little surprise when he suffered his third defeat in four years, but it was nevertheless a glorious defeat.

Suleiman Nyambui of Tanzania outkicked Steve to win the 3,000m in 7:43.12 to Ovett's 7:43.87, the fastest time by a Briton for four years. Ovett showed he had regained both strength and stamina in a run which Cliff Temple succinctly described as 'significantly insignificant'. Yet the back pages of the following morning's Sunday papers seemed to gloat over his defeat, bearing headlines such as 'Agony for Ovett in Oslo', 'Misery — Ovett's Oslo shocker' and so on.

Ovett naturally lacked his old blistering sprint finish, but that was hardly surprising considering he only had a few months of training under his belt following a major operation. Despite the criticisms of the popular Press, it was in fact another brilliant performance by Ovett, who said after the race: 'Of course I never like to be beaten but I was perfectly happy with the time and the way the race went.'

Four days later, the Steve Ovett of old took the stage for a 2,000m test in Budapest and provided the perfect retort to his many detractors. After looking a lot more smooth and comfortable with the almost pedestrian early pace than he had done in Oslo, he moved confidently on to Craig Masback's shoulder when the American made a break 50 yards before the bell. As the leaders rounded the final turn, Australia's Mike Hillardt moved ominously on to Ovett's shoulder, but the Brighton man zipped into overdrive and gained a clear ten yards lead within a couple of seconds. There were no waves to the crowd before Ovett crossed the line first in 5:05:75 but this seemed more like a vintage Ovett performance.

The promised Crystal Palace 3,000m on July 17th began to look at lot more interesting. All 17,000 seats had been snapped up and the AAA were seriously considering installing a 2,000 seater temporary stand to cope with demand until fate once again intervened to prevent another Ovett-Coe confrontation. On July 5th, Coe confirmed growing speculation that his right leg had suffered a stress bone fracture and pulled out of the Crystal Palace race.

'It has been a bit of a sickener and people may feel I've let them down, but I did not want this to happen,' said Coe. Having sold TV rights all around the world, the AAA were 'bitterly disappointed' by Coe's withdrawal — but perhaps not quite as disappointed as Ovett.

Upon being informed of Coe's withdrawal by Andy Norman, Ovett's reply was described as 'unprintable' and 'a little stronger than disappointed' by Norman. Ovett later said: 'After my injury I could have quite easily gone through this season saying,"It's only the Europeans, I've won them before," and settle back to think about next year. These three races with Coe gave me the incentive to come back. I'm very disapponted. I've done a lot of work and made a lot of sacrifices to get fit for the 3,000m race.'

Unlike the 1980 Golden Mile, however, the Crystal Palace 3,000m didn't lose all of its sparkle because of Coe's absence. Critics had remarked from the day the race was announced that Ovett and Coe wouldn't be the only prospective victors. Few of the general sporting public agreed — until the evening of Wednesday July 7th when the cream of the world's athletic talent once again descended on the compact Bislett Stadium for the Oslo Games.

Ovett broke his own British 2,000m record by 0.11 of a second. Looking comfortable all of the way, he moved up a gear around the final turn and left Tom Wessinghage standing, easing across the line in 4:57.71. The world 1500m record holder was looking in better shape with every outing, but on this occasion he was a long way short of being the hero of the Oslo crowd. Steve Scott had earlier torn apart a strong field to take over from Ovett as the second fastest ever miler. Clocking 3:47.69 — 0.71 of a second faster than Ovett's best — Scott's run was quite a devastating performance and an agonising 0.36 of a second short of Coe's record. The pre-season feeling that Ovett and Coe no longer held a stranglehold on world middle distance running was beginning to be justified.

No sooner had Ovett answered Scott's blistering run

with his new British 2,000m record than the capacity Norwegian crowd witnessed the greatest athletic feat since Bob Beamon leapt out of the record books and into the realms of legend in the 1968 Olympic long jump.

Dave Moorcroft had slipped almost too quietly into the shadows when — despite winning the Commonwealth Games 1500m title in 1978 — he failed to make any impression on Ovett and Coe's middle distance domination in 1978 and 1979. Seeking solace in the 5,000m, Moorcroft's Olympic chances were upset by 'Moscow tummy' but he won the 1981 Europa Cup 5,000m final despite being injured. It was, however, a rather different Dave Moorcroft who had already underlined his intentions for the season by smashing his best mile time with a 3:49.34 run for third place in the Dream Mile on June 26th.

Henry Rono's world 5,000m record had looked one of the best in the books and it therefore stunned the athletics world when quiet Moorcroft from Coventry left the Kenyan half a lap behind as he reduced the record by almost six seconds. In one of the most devastating displays of front running ever seen, Moorcroft covered the twelve and a half lap distance an amazing 20 seconds faster than ever before to set a new world record of 13 minutes 00.42 seconds. Ovett and Coe were no longer the undisputed kings of British athletics. As Ken Mays observed in the *Daily Telegraph*, 'For the first time in his life, Ovett was completely overshadowed on a track where he has become a national hero.'

The Crystal Palace 3,000m was clearly not going to be an anti-climax after all. Moreover, had Coe been fit, neither he nor Ovett would have started the race as favourite — that was Moorcroft, quite clearly, now dubbed, 'the Third Man of British athletics' by the Press. With Ovett forging his way back to form and Moorcroft and Scott in world beating form, the 3,000m began to look a very interesting race. But, once again, there was another twist of fate to come before the July 17th date.

Ovett collapsed during a 1500m race in Paris and was

rushed to hospital. The drama occurred after three laps when Ovett was trailing well behind Kenya's Mike Boit and it was the first time he had ever dropped out of a race. With his wife and Andy Norman in close attendance, Ovett was stretchered out of the stadium and taken to hospital with suspected appendicitis.

Ovett's complaint was later diagnosed as colic (from which his father suffers), but initial fears that he wouldn't be able to run at Crystal Palace were soon allayed. 'I'm only 70 to 80 per cent fit, apart from the breathing trouble I had in Paris,' he said. 'My right leg still tires faster than the good one. It's a bit like driving with a flat tyre, but I can't pull out now. I've had to move heaven and earth to get ready for this one.'

Ovett clearly knew he wasn't in good shape and he never looked comfortable on July 17th as Moorcroft pushed the pace hard up front. Red faced and with obvious breathing difficulties, Ovett attempted to keep in touch with the pace over the opening three or four laps but eventually trailed home tenth in the respectable time of 7 mins 48.07 — Moorcroft having won in a European Record of 7:32.79. While Moorcroft milked the applause of the crowd, Ovett slumped dejectedly to the ground in the inner track area.

Moorcroft's first reaction at the post race press conference poignantly summed up Ovett's race. 'Where did Steve finish?' he asked reporters. 'Oh, really! Well, I thought he could either win it or come last. He's a winner. He's not particularly good at coming second or third and I thought in this sort of race that if he wasn't in there to win, then he'd find it difficult to come fourth or whatever.

'That's not a criticism; that's what makes him so good. You saw it in the Olympic 1500m final — once Seb was away, he lost interest and concentration. I think he's done remarkably well to get back the way he has. It was probably asking too much of him tonight. That's the first time I've beaten him since the semi-finals of the Olympic 1500m in 1976.'

While the super-fit Moorcroft had stolen the limelight

from the obviously unfit Ovett and the injured Coe, the 'Fourth Man of British athletics' began to emerge. Steve Cram had sensibly chosen to build up his season slowly and quietly following his early season injury, but half an hour before the 3,000m race the 21-year-old Geordie at last moved on to the same level as Ovett, Coe and Moorcroft.

Most observers agreed that the one chink in Cram's armour during the two or three preceding seasons had been his lack of a comparable blistering sprint finish to Ovett or Coe. But he proved this to be no real handicap by running the fastest 800m of 1982, 1 minute 44.45 seconds, in a supremely confident front running display. It left one in little doubt that the miling confrontation everyone wanted to see was now Ovett v Coe v Cram, the latter now installed as favourite to win the European 1500m title. Cram's time was the third fastest ever by a Briton, behind Coe's 1:41.73 and Ovett's 1:44.09.

'I think Ovett and Coe can no longer consider themselves as having a divine right to win races,' said Cram. 'It's not just me — there's Scott, Maree and Moorcroft. Unless Seb and Steve are in real top form, they're going to find it difficult to win whereas previously they were so much better than anybody else that they could have an off night and still win. The gap has closed.'

In Ovett's absence — he was awaiting the results of a series of medical tests — Cram easily won the AAA Championship 1500m title in 3:36.4 before launching a verbal attack at the selectors for keeping major games places open for both Ovett and Coe. 'They should treat Ovett and Coe the same as everyone else,' said Cram. 'Why should we wait for them? If I hadn't been fit to run today I wonder if they would have kept a place open for me. The myth of Steve and Seb's invincibility has gone now. We need more openness from them over their progress with illness and injury, especially from Seb. Steve has made a big effort this year and a hell of a lot of sacrifices, despite his problems, but I think Seb has kept us all a little in the dark.'

Despite his fitness problems, Ovett was controversially selected to run both the 1500m and the 800m for England at the Commonwealth Games in Brisbane; his choice in the 800m causing a major furore in the Press. Rotherham's Peter Elliott had been overlooked by the selectors, despite trimming 0.16 of a second from Ovett's UK teenage record in winning the AAA's 800m title ahead of John Walker and Chris McGeorge in 1:45.61. The race had been billed as a trial and the Press, Elliott himself and a great number of people within the athletics world were convinced that he, and not Ovett, should have been picked.

Sebastian Coe and Garry Cook were considered to be automatic selecti ıs and Elliott quite rightly believed that his AAA's win had won him the third place in the English team. The answer Ovett and Andy Norman gave to their many critics was both calculated and shrewd. Bowing to pressure to prove his fitness, Ovett chose to run against Elliott for England over 800m at Edinburgh the following Saturday (31st July). Hence, when Ovett comfortably stuck to Elliott's shoulder before pouncing on the final bend to ease over the line in 1:47.59, three strides clear of Elliot, the argument appeared to have been settled. Ovett, at least, thought as much. Stopping in his stride at the line, he stared icily at the Meadowbank Press Box for what must have been half-a-minute before punching his right fist into the air.

This action, pointed out Ken Mays in the *Daily Telegraph,* left Andy Norman, England's Commonwealth Games team manager, 'almost gloating with satisfaction.' Mays added: 'Mr Norman, who in his part-time capacity handles the English side of athletics in a way that would do the secret service credit, had been under a misapprehension all week, for it was not Ovett's selection for Brisbane that was heavily criticised, but the way he handled it. Unfortunately, it appears that Ovett also got the wrong impression. Though his relationship with the English Press has never been a close one, once more he refused to attend a conference to at least let the public know his feelings of last week.'

Ovett no doubt felt that the manner of his victory, together with his rather pronounced post-race gesture, expressed his feelings louder than any words could have done. Elliott himself conceded: 'Although I was sick at the way I had been treated, I'm now very much happier. I know in my own mind Steve is the better runner. It was great while it lasted and I know I had a lot of people on my side, but it's all over now and I hope everyone will now forget the fuss of the last few days.' They certainly didn't. But when the fuss eventually died down most people agreed that the selectors were guilty of acting unfairly in the way they ignored the result of what was advertised as a selection trial.

As the 1982 track season began to gather momentum, controversy followed controversy for the two almost forgotten heroes of 1977, 1978, 1979, 1980 and 1981.

Coe, who had announced his withdrawal from the proposed 800m clash in Nice, bounced back from injury on August 4th to achieve the European qualifying standard for 800m in a specially arranged secret meeting at Nottingham's Harvey Hadden Stadium. Ovett protested that Coe had been given an unfair advantage, as he had been forced into running the qualifying time at the BAAB's Golden Jubilee Games at Crystal Palace three days later. The British Board then threatened to disqualify Coe's time if he refused to run in the meeting. They claimed that the sponsors and TV were angered by the fact that Coe could run in front of no spectators, but not in a major meeting in front of a packed Crystal Palace crowd.

Coe refused to run, saying it was unfair to put pressure on him to compete in front of a large crowd when he was still recovering from injury and in danger of breaking down. After reportedly threatening to boycott the meeting in response to Coe's reaction, Ovett eventually ran in the 1500m and did enough to ensure his selection for the European Championships. He won in 3:38.48 from Gateshead's Geoff Turnbull, who gave the world record holder a tough time on the last lap until Ovett glided past him 80 metres from the tape.

The following Wednesday (August 11th), Ovett was beaten into second place by West German 400m hurdler Harald Schmid over 800m in Viareggio, Italy. Ovett had broken clear of Schmid and Chris McGeorge along the final straight, only for Schmid to burst past both Britons and cross the line first in 1:45.90. Ovett held on to second place in 1:46.08 — his fastest 800m since his Olympic victory — with McGeorge third in 1:46.70. After the meeting, American race promoter Scott Fengelly told Pressmen that Ovett and Coe would definitely meet in the scheduled mile race in Eugene, despite their injury and fitness problems.

No sooner had the public began to anticipate the sporting clash of the century than the inevitable happened once again. Three days later the whole of Ovett's season was thrown into turmoil when he pulled a hamstring during a training session at Brighton's Withdean Stadium. Following a week of speculation about whether Ovett would be fit for Athens, he finally decided to bring down the curtain on his most patchy track season to date and withdrew from both the European Championships and the Commonwealth Games.

Eight years of spiralling higher and higher towards the very pinnacle of athletics glory had come to an end — at least a temporary one — for Ovett. Steve Cram went on impressively to capture the 1500m gold medals in Athens and Brisbane, while Coe proved that he — like Ovett — is human after all when he was defeated by a hitherto unheard of West German, Hans Peter Ferner, in the European Championships 800m final. The seemingly invincible middle distance kings of the past four seasons had been dethroned. Cram, at just 21, had acceded to that throne.

The Ovett-Coe saga, one of the most curious and enthralling chapters in the history of world athletics, has now come to an end. The inaugural World Athletics Championships in August 1983, with the prospect of a three-way British contest in the 1500m final, could represent an intriguing opening chapter in the Ovett-Coe-Cram battle for world middle distance running supremacy.

One is loath to make any rash predictions, but Ovett and Coe's year of experiencing the 'other' side of athletics should ensure that they return to action mentally tougher and more determined in 1983. And the Cram they will come up against will be a far more confident and capable runner than they last encountered. One thing is for sure: the end of the Ovett-Coe story promises to herald an exciting new drama.

At the time of writing (November 1982), Ovett is at last back in training after his many injuries and setbacks of the previous twelve months and he has already declared his main objectives for 1983. In an attempt to regain some of the strength he has lost through injury in 1982, Ovett intends to become involved in the cross country season for the first time in four years — his aim being to win the English title at Luton and the World Championships at Gateshead.

After that comes the intriguing 1983 track season, with the prospect of Ovett, Coe and Cram meeting in spiked combat for the first time since the 1980 Olympic 1500m final in Moscow. Cram and Ovett will certainly be aiming for the 1500m gold medal at the inaugural IAAF World Athletics Championships in Helsinki, but it remains to be seen whether Coe — whose burning ambition remains to win a major games 800m gold medal — will choose to compete in the metric mile.

Quite a widespread feeling exists in the athletics world that Ovett's hunger for athletics glory has been blunted by his recent troubles and that he is, in any case, past his best. To those Doubting Thomases, Ovett sounded a clear warning at the end of the ITV documentary profile which was broadcast in September 1982.

'In a way, I'm glad about the past few months,' he said. 'In the past I had things easy, just drifting along and never being pushed to the limit. Being injured has made me sit back and take a good look at my running, and I know I'll be better than ever before in 1983. I know a lot of people are saying Ovett is finished but they're going to get a shock next year. I'll be back, more ruthless and determined than ever before. There's still a lot more to come.'

While the story of Steve Ovett the athlete had reached a most interesting stage, the story of Steve Ovett the man behind the brash facade began to develop quite significantly in 1982. Following the publication of the hardback edition of this book in April, Ovett started to make up for all of his violently publicity shy years; though I hasten to add that such a change was purely coincidental.

Several months of Ovett's increasing emergence into the public eye culminated in the hour-long documentary, 'Ovett', which charted the athlete's frustrating progress from injury to injury during the previous nine months. Producer Adrian Metcalfe and director John Sheppard had planned to film a record of Ovett's build up from midwinter training to the anticipated triumphs on the European circuit and at the European Championships. Instead the programme developed into a fascinating chronicle of Ovett's first struggling period in athletics for eight years.

'This year has taught me a lot,' said Ovett. 'I used to think winning was everything. Being injured has made me appreciate the other side of the coin.'

The programme also shed light on Steve Ovett's rapidly changing public image. For someone who claimed to be indifferent to the Press, Ovett has certainly given the matter of his relations with the media a great deal of consideration. It had always seemed that Ovett's decision to 'take on' the media was a further outlet for Ovett the fickle and ruthless track runner. And during the documentary he admitted: 'I've toyed with the idea of imagery with the media by giving them certain things and not giving them other things. It's been fascinating.'

In other words, Steve Ovett fed the media a distorted

image, and they in turn could not be completely blamed for passing on that distortion to Joe Public, as mentioned previously. But Ovett had tired of this long-running charade and was ready to open up.

ITV chiefs weren't too happy with him when he appeared on BBC TV during the week leading up to their documentary, analysing the events of the European Championships from a London studio. Ovett, a man who often professed to feeling profoundly uncomfortable in the limelight, came across remarkably well and when he returned to the TV studios for the Commonwealth Games programmes he proved beyond doubt that he is easily the most competent sporting guest analyst adopted by TV in recent years. A natural he most certainly was, and can no doubt look forward to a long and profitable future in television.

A similar prospect faces him in the sportswear business. In October 1982 the sportswear firm 'Ovett Ltd', Ovett being the major shareholder and one of five directors, was launched. Any money accruing from the business will be held in a BAAB trust fund until Ovett eventually retires from athletics. Ovett, who at one time appeared to be lagging well behind Coe in the commercial athletics race, had surged into the lead.

And, to complete a year in which the old Steve Ovett seemed to fade into obscurity, the British athletics Press were invited to re-unite with their greatest foe at the press conference to launch his business, amid the plush surroundings of the Waldorf Hotel. 'Ovett ends cold war,' read one typical newspaper headline the next morning.

'The old barriers are gradually breaking down,' Ovett told the Press. 'Through the ITV documentary and my other TV appearances, the general public realise I am not the menacing character they believed me to be. I am reaching the stage where I feel I can now give something back. As athletes, we have to remember we are in one of the most popular spectator sports and we have a responsibility to keep things going.'

Some of the Press understandably found Ovett's new stance rather difficult to accept, pointing out that it was quite a coincidence that his change of heart coincided with his need to promote a commercial enterprise. 'Could it not be conceivable that he now needs publicity for the sake of his bank balance?' commented one columnist. Nevertheless, the general Press reception was rather more favourable. A new range of Ovett adjectives were suddenly adopted. Words such as 'brash', 'arrogant' and 'immature' were replaced by 'cordial', 'lucid' and 'articulate'. Indeed, one national newspaper observed: 'Goodness and light beamed from him. This was a brand new, sparkling Steve Ovett.'

It was left to *Mail on Sunday* columnist Pat Collins, perhaps the only journalist to really get near to the real Steve Ovett in the past, to once again provide a perceptive understanding of what he called 'Ovett's media face-lift.' Collins pointed out that Ovett now sensed the affection of the public was leaning towards him rather than Coe. The situation had changed because of the attempt to prolong Coe's unbelievably nice — with a capital N — media image by taking part in embarrasingly self-effacing TV adverts, something which 'faintly amused Ovett'.

'The public has always known that I was never the beast that I was painted and Seb was never the saint some people made him out to be,' Ovett told Collins. 'Little things stuck in their minds, things that maybe the Press never even noticed. That business on the rostrum in Moscow, when I'd won the Olympic 800 and Seb seemed to be struggling with himself before he could bring himself to shake hands with me. I knew how he felt and I knew how disappointed he was, but it didn't go down too well with the general public.

'I think, too, that I got a lot of sympathy from people who believed I was getting a bad deal from the Press. Sometimes it hurt me, when I knew the criticism was really unfair. But I lived with it because there wasn't much else I could do about it. But now it's changing. I don't know why, because I don't know how it got so bad in the first place.

'I think things will be easier from now on. Perhaps we're all becoming more mature. I know I feel competent to handle the kind of situations which my experience prevented me from handling before.I've got to start getting involved because I owe it to the sport. But that's just being realistic — don't think I've started to worry about my image.'

Collins went on to make perhaps the most pertinent point of the whole Ovett-Coe melodrama. 'There they are, the finest middle-distance runners of our time; the finest, indeed, of all time,' he wrote. 'And all we can do, Press and public alike, is probe their personalities, examine their motives and balance them on an eternal see-saw. We find it impossible to believe that we can possess two men who happen to be both talented and engaging. Naturally, they affect to ignore our impertinence. But they are wounded and puzzled, and every so often they find the words to express their bewilderment.'

As we await the 1983 World Championships and the 1984 Olympics and reflect on the Steve Ovett story so far, it is perhaps fitting to conclude this portrait with the words Ovett recently chose to express that bewilderment.

'People like Seb and me, we're built up to the point where ultimately we can do nothing but fail,' he said. 'I do get injured. Seb does occasionally get beaten. It happens. And it happens because we're only human beings. Is that so difficult to understand?'

Statistical Appendix

Details of all Steve Ovett's track races since 1970

Statistics compiled by Dave Cocksedge and Simon Turnbull of the National Union of Track Statisticians and Steve's former coach Barry Tilbury.

APPENDIX

Listed below are details of Steve Ovett's track races since 1970.

1970 (age fourteen)

Date	Meeting/Track	Event	Position	Performance
5 Apr.	– Crawley	800m	1st	2:09.0
18 Apr.	– Epsom	800m	1st	2:07.0
25 Apr.	– Brighton	800m	1st	2:01.6
3 May	– Crawley	800m	1st	2:00.1
16 May	– Walton	800m	1st	2:00.0
18 May	Brighton Schools' Champs. – Brighton	800m	1st	2:04.0
21 May	Brighton Schools' Champs. – Brighton	400m	1st	52.2
3 Jun.	– Crystal Palace	800m	2nd	2:02.9
13 Jun.	Sussex Schools' Champs. – Brighton	400m	1st	51.6
14 Jun.	– Aldershot	100m	1st	11.9
14 Jun.	– Aldershot	200m	1st	23.8
28 Jun.	Young Athletes Meeting – Thurrock	100m	1st	11.9
28 Jun.	Young Athletes Meeting – Thurrock	200m	1st	24.1
10 Jul.	English Schools' Champs. – Solihull	400m-heat	1st	52.7
10 Jul.	English Schools' Champs. – Solihull	400m-semi	3rd	53.7
11 Jul.	English Schools' Champs. – Solihull	400m-final	1st	51.8
15 Jul.	– Crawley	800m	1st	2:09.0
15 Jul.	– Crawley	100m	1st	11.8
21 Jul.	– Crawley	800m	1st	2:07.0
21 Jul.	– Crawley	100m	1st	12.2

Date	Meeting/Track	Event	Position	Performance
6 Aug.	– Brighton	200m	1st	24.2
9 Aug.	– Crawley	1500m	1st	4:43.0
9 Aug.	– Crawley	800m	1st	2:18.0
9 Aug.	– Crawley	L. Jump	1st	20′ 02½″
15 Aug.	– Feltham	400m	3rd	52.4
22 Aug.	– Epsom	200m	1st	24.1
23 Aug.	– Crystal Palace	400m	6th	52.6
30 Aug.	– Walton	100m	4th	12.1
30 Aug.	– Walton	200m	3rd	24.3
5 Sept.	– Brighton	400m	1st	51.9
5 Sept.	– Brighton	L. Jump	1st	20′ 06″
9 Sept.	– Walton	400m	1st	53.7

1971 (age fifteen)

Date	Meeting/Track	Event	Position	Performance
18 Apr.	– Maidenhead	1500m	1st	4:17.6
24 Apr.	– Brighton	800m	1st	2:01.3
1 May	Pollitt Trophy – Brighton	800m	2nd	1:56.8
19 May	– Crystal Palace	800m	1st	1:57.8
27 May	Brighton Schools' Champs. – Brighton	400m	1st	51.5
5 Jun.	Sussex County Champs. – Crawley	800m	1st	1:59.3
5 Jun.	Sussex County Champs. – Crawley	400m	1st	53.8
19 Jun.	Southern Youth Champs. – Crystal Palace	800m-heat	2nd	1:59.9
20 Jun.	Southern Youth Champs. – Crystal Palace	800m-final	5th	2:00.9
22 Jun.	– Brighton	100m	1st	12.0
26 Jun.	– Brighton	400m	1st	51.3

Date	Meeting/Track	Event	Position	Performance
9 Jul.	English Schools' Champs. – Crystal Palace	400m-heat	2nd	51.7
10 Jul.	English Schools' Champs. – Crystal Palace	400m-semi	1st	50.4
10 Jul.	English Schools' Champs. – Crystal Palace	400m-final	3rd	50.4
17 Jul.	– Brighton	100m	2nd	12.1
17 Jul.	– Brighton	200m	1st	23.7
20 Jul.	– Brighton	200m	1st	23.5
20 Jul.	– Brighton	L. Jump	1st	20′ 07″
20 Jul.	– Brighton	H. Jump	1st	5′ 05″
24 Jul.	– Brighton	400m	1st	51.1
24 Jul.	– Brighton	L. Jump	1st	20′ 07″
24 Jul.	– Brighton	H. Jump	1st	5′ 03″
25 Jul.	– Crawley	400m-relay	–	49.8
28 Jul.	– Crystal Palace	400m	1st	50.0
31 Jul.	– Brighton	400m-relay	–	49.8
7 Aug.	AAA Youths Champs. – Wolverhampton	400m	1st	49.8
23.5 at 200m.				
14 Aug.	– Bracknell	400m-relay	–	49.7
18 Aug.	– Crystal Palace	400m	2nd	51.8
22 Aug.	Invitation Meeting – Crystal Palace	800m	1st	1:55.3*
**UK age fourteen record.*				
22 Aug.	Invitation Meeting – Crystal Palace	400m-relay	1st	50.0

1972 (age sixteen)

Date	Meeting/Track	Event	Position	Performance
19 Mar.	– Crystal Palace	1000m	1st	2:34.5
20 Mar.	– Crystal Palace	1000m	1st	2:29.2
26 Apr.	Newham Games – Newham	600m	2nd	1:19.5
1st – M. Winbolt Lewis 1:18.7				
10 Jun.	Sussex County Champs. – Brighton	800m	1st	1:53.3
10 Jun.	Sussex County Champs. – Brighton	1500m	1st	4:09.7
17 Jun.	Sussex Schools' Champs. – Brighton	800m	1st	1:52.5
7 Jul.	English Schools' Champs. – Washington	800m-heat	1st	2:00.2
8 Jul.	English Schools' Champs. – Washington	800m-final	1st	1:55.0
22 Jul.	AAA Youth Champs. – Kirkby	400m-heat	1st	50.9
23 Jul.	AAA Youth Champs. – Kirkby	400m-final	1st	49.1
– Aug.	Southend Club Match – West Germany	400m	1st	48.9
– Aug.	Southend Club Match – West Germany	800m	1st	1:53.6
20 Aug.	Youth Invitational Meeting – Crystal Palace	400m	1st	48.4*
**UK Youth record*				
20 Aug.	Youth Invitational Meeting – Crystal Palace	400m-relay	1st	49.4
10 Sept.	– Newham	1500m	1st	4:01.5
20 Sept.	SCAAA Open Meeting – Crystal Palace	200m	2nd	23.0
1st – G. Doerr 22.9				
20 Sept.	SCAAA Open Meeting – Crystal Palace	400m	1st	50.8

1973 (age seventeen)

Date	Meeting/Track	Event	Position	Performance
2 May	Golden Wonder Floodlit Meeting – Newham	600m	1st	1:20.0
19 May	Sussex County Champs. – Brighton	1500m	1st	3:53.4

Date	Meeting/Track	Event	Position	Performance
23 May	– Crystal Palace	400m-relay	2nd	47.6
Alan Pascoe 46.8				
27 May	Inter Counties Champs. – Warley	400m-heat	4th	48.0
28 May	Inter Counties Champs. – Warley	400m-final	6th	48.4
1st – J. Aukett 46.9				
2 Jun.	– Newham	200m	1st	22.8
2 Jun.	– Newham	800m	1st	1:54.4
15 Jun.	SCAAA Junior Champs. – Crystal Palace	1500m-heat	1st	4:04.2
16 Jun.	SCAAA Junior Champs. – Crystal Palace	1500m-final	1st	3:51.6
22 Jun.	Southern Champs. – Crystal Palace	800m-heat	1st	1:57.0
23 Jun.	Southern Champs. – Crystal Palace	800m-final	2nd	1:48.4
1st – P. Browne 1:48.3				
13 Jul.	AAA Champs. – Crystal Palace	800m-heat	2nd	1:47.5
1st – M. Winzenreid 1:47.3				
14 Jul.	AAA Champs. – Crystal Palace	800m-final	6th	1:47.3
1st – A. Carter 1:45.1				
25 Jul.	City Charity Meeting – Motspur Park	Mile	2nd	4:00.0
1st – N. Rose 3:58.4				
4 Aug.	UK 'A' v France 'A' – Scottville, France	800m	3rd	1:49.6
1st – Sanchez 1:48.9				
17 Aug.	London Fire Brigade Meeting – Crystal Palace	1000m	1st	2:20.0
19 Aug.	Junior Area Match – Crystal Palace	1500m	1st	3:55.7
24 Aug.	European Junior Champs. – Duisburg, W.Germany	800m-heat	1st	1:51.6
25 Aug.	European Junior Champs. – Duisburg, W. Germany	800m-semi	1st	1:49.6
26 Aug.	European Junior Champs. – Duisburg, W. Germany	800m-final	1st	1:47.5
2nd Wulbeck; 3rd Gohlke; 4th Van Damme				

Date	Meeting/Track	Event	Position	Performance
14 Sept.	IAC/Coca Cola Meeting – Crystal Palace	Mile	9th	4:09.2
1st – B. J. Jipcho 3:56.2				
19 Sept.	UK v Sweden Junior International – Warley	1500m	1st	3:54.9
29 Sept.	England Commonwealth Games – Crystal Palace	800m	3rd	1:48.4
1st – C. Campbell 1:48.0				
	1974 (age eighteen)			
12 Jan.	MCAAA Indoor Meeting – RAF Cosford	800m	1st	1:52.8
Ovett contracted glandular fever				
1 Jun.	British League Meeting – Edinburgh	800m	1st	1:53.7
1 Jun.	British League Meeting – Edinburgh	1500m	1st	3:46.2
15 Jun.	SCAAA Junior Champs. – Crystal Palace	400m-heat	1st	49.7
15 Jun.	SCAAA Junior Champs. – Crystal Palace	400m-final	1st	47.5
21 Jun.	Southern Champs. – Crystal Palace	800m-heat	1st	1:52.7
22 Jun.	Southern Champs. – Crystal Palace	800m-final	1st	1:47.6
30 Jun.	UK v Poland v Canada – Warsaw	800m	1st	1:46.8
12 Jul.	AAA Champs. – Crystal Palace	800m-heat	1st	1:48.8
13 Jul.	AAA Champs. – Crystal Palace	800m-final	1st	1:46.9
17 Jul.	– Haringey	Brigg Mile	1st	3:59.4
27 Jul.	UK v Czechoslovakia – Edinburgh	800m	1st	1:48.8
3 Aug.	Gateshead Games	1000m	2nd	2:20.1
1st – A. Carter 2:18.5				
10 Aug.	– Crystal Palace	Mile	5th	4:03.8
1st – F. Clement 3:57.4				
2 Sept.	European Champs. – Rome	800m-heat	2nd	1:47.0
1st – G. Ghipu 1:46.9				

Date	Meeting/Track	Event	Position	Performance
3 Sept.	European Champs. – Rome	800m-semi	1st	1:47.2
4 Sept.	European Champs. – Rome	800m-final	2nd	1:45.77
1st – L. Susanj 1:44.1				
	1975 (age nineteen)			
31 Jan	AAA Indoor Championships – Cosford	1500m-heat	1st	3:48.9
1 Feb.	AAA Indoor Championships – Cosford	1500m-final	5th	3:45.9
1st – P. Banning 3:42.6				
17 May	National League Meeting – Brighton	1500m	1st	3:54.6
31 May	– Crystal Palace	Emsley Carr Mile	6th	4:00.1
1st – F. Bayi 3:55.5				
21 Jun.	UK v GDR – Dresden	800m	3rd	1:47.6
1st – H. Ohlert 1:47.0				
22 Jun.	UK v GDR – Dresden	1500m	2nd	3:43.3
1st – H. Ohlert 3:42.1				
30 Jun.	Invitation Meeting – Stockholm	Mile	9th	3:57.0
1st – J. Walker 3:52.2				
4 Jul.	Invitation Meeting – Crystal Palace	800m	3rd	1.49.3
1st – M. Boit 1:48.6				
5 July	National League Meeting – Kirkby	400m	1st	48.7
5 Jul.	National League Meeting – Kirkby	800m	1st	1:52.3
13 Jul.	Europa Cup semi-final – Crystal Palace	800m	1st	1:46.7
26 Jul.	National League Meeting – Barking	200m	1st	21.7*
doubtful time, more accurately 22.7				
26 July	National League Meeting – Barking	400m	1st	48.7

Date	Meeting/Track	Event	Position	Performance
1 Aug.	AAA Championships – Crystal Palace	800m-heat	1st	1:49.5
2 Aug.	AAA Champs. – Crystal Palace	800m-final	1st	1:46.1
7 Aug.	SCAAA Open Meeting – Crystal Palace	800m	1st	1:47.7
17 Aug.	Europa Cup Final – Nice	800m	1st	1:46.6
19 Aug.	Invitation Meeting – Stockholm	1500m	9th	3:45.9
1st – J. Walker 3:35.6				
29 Aug.	Coca Cola Meeting – Crystal Palace	Mile	8th	4:01.3
1st – J Walker 3:53.6 (Ovett's last mile loss for six years)				
1 Sept.	Manitou Games – Gateshead	300m	6th	35.3
1st – D. Jenkins 32.9				
	1976 (age twenty)			
12 May	SCAAA Open Meeting – Crystal Palace	600m	1st	1:18.5
12 May	SCAAA Open Meeting – Crystal Palace	400m	1st	48.9
15 May	– Crawley	400m	1st	49.0
22 May	– Liverpool	800m	1st	1:52.7
26 May	Borough Rd. Coll. v AAA Meeting – Crystal Palace	400m	7th	48.63
30 May	Inter-Counties Champs. – Crystal Palace	800m-heat	1st	1:51.7
31 May	Inter-Counties Champs. – Crystal Palace	800m-final	1st	1:47.3
4 Jun.	Olympic trials – Crystal Palace	800m-heat	1st	1:48.6
5 Jun.	Olympic trials – Crystal Palace	800m-final	1st	1:46.7
11 Jun.	Olympic trials – Crystal Palace	1500m-heat	3rd	3:44.4
12 Jun.	Olympic trials – Crystal Palace	1500m-final	1st	3:39.6
18 Jun.	Southern Champs. – Crystal Palace	400m-heat	1st	49.0
19 Jun.	Southern Champs. – Crystal Palace	400m-final	4th	48.17
27 Jun.	Invitation Meeting – Saarijarvi, Finland	800m	1st	1:50.1

Date	Meeting/Track	Event	Position	Performance
3 Jul.	UK v Poland v Canada – Crystal Palace	800m	1st	1:46.7
23 Jul.	Olympic Games – Montreal	800m-heat	1st	1:48.3
24 Jul.	Olympic Games – Montreal	800m-semi	3rd	1:46.1
1st – Juantorena 1:45.9; 2nd – Van Damme 1:46.0				
25 Jul.	Olympic Games – Montreal	800m-final	5th	1:45.4
1st – Juantorena 1:43.5; 2nd – Van Damme 1:43.86; 3rd – Wolhunter 1:44.12; 4th – Wulbeck 1:45.26				
29 Jul.	Olympic Games – Montreal	1500m-heat	1st	3:37.9
30 Jul.	Olympic Games – Montreal	1500m-semi	5th	3:40.3
1st – J. Walker 3:39.65				
6 Aug.	IAC/Coca Cola Meeting – Edinburgh	800m	1st	1:46.9
7 Aug.	Open Meeting – Coatbridge	1000m	1st	2:21.0
10 Aug.	Invitation Meeting – Helsinki	800m	2nd	1:46.1
13 Aug.	AAA Champs. – Crystal Palace	800m-heat	1st	1:50.0
14 Aug.	AAA Champs. – Crystal Palace	800m-final	1st	1:47.3
16 Aug.	Invitation Meeting – Nice	1000m	2nd	2:19.2
18 Aug.	Invitation Meeting – Zurich	800m	2nd	1:45.5
21 Aug.	– Edinburgh	800m	1st	1:48.2

1977 (age twenty-one)

Date	Meeting/Track	Event	Position	Performance
30 Apr.	National League Meeting – Brighton	800m	1st	1:53.9
30 Apr.	National League Meeting – Brighton	1500m	1st	4:04.0
30 Apr.	National League Meeting – Brighton	3000m	1st	8:18.8
13 May	Invitation Meeting – Kingston, Jamaica	1500m	2nd	3:39.8
1st – S. Scott 3:39.8 – Ovett's last 1500m loss for four seasons				
18 May	Philips Night of Athletes – Crystal Palace	3000m	2nd	7:53.4
1st – F. Bayi				

Date	Meeting/Track	Event	Position	Performance
21 May	National League Meeting – Brighton	1500m	1st	3:53.4
21 May	National League Meeting – Brighton	400m-relay	–	48.5
28 May	– Belfast	Mile	1st	3:56.2
1 Jun.	– St. Maur	1500m	1st	3:39.8
12 Jun.	UK Champs. – Cwmbran	1500m	1st	3:37.5
26 Jun.	– Crystal Palace	Mile	1st	3:54.7*
**UK record*				
2 Jul.	British League Meeting – Keele	1500m	1st	3:52.0
2 Jul.	British League Meeting – Keele	400m-relay	–	48.3
5 Jul.	Invitation Meeting – Cork	Mile	1st	3:59.1
7 Jul.	Invitation Meeting – Middleton, Eire	5000m	1st	
16 Jul.	European Cup semi-final – Crystal Palace	1500m	1st	3:39.1
30 Jul.	Gateshead Games	5000m	2nd	13:25.0
1st – M. Yifter				
4 Aug.	– Bideford	800m	1st	1:58.1
4 Aug.	– Bideford	1500m	1st	3:50.0
4 Aug.	– Bideford	3000m	1st	8:22.2
13 Aug.	European Cup Final – Helsinki	1500m	1st	3:44.9
20 Aug.	Half-marathon – Dartford	13.2 miles	1st	65:38
29 Aug.	– Crystal Palace	800m	1st	1:48.3
3 Sept.	World Cup – Dusseldorf	1500m	1st	3:34.5*
**UK record*				
9 Sept.	IAC/Coca Cola Meeting – Crystal Palace	Mile	1st	3:56.6
23 Sept.	Invitation Meeting – Wattenscheid	3000m	1st	7:41.3
24 Sept.	Invitation Meeting – Hanover	2000m	2nd	5:04.7
1st – T. Wessinghage				

1978 (age twenty-two)

Date	Meeting/Track	Event	Position	Performance
29 Apr.	– Brighton	1500m	1st	3:59.7
29 Apr.	– Brighton	3000m	1st	8:16.6
3 May	– Crystal Palace	3000m	1st	7:57.8
6 May	– Hendon	1500m	1st	3:52.2
6 May	– Hendon	1500m	1st	3:52.2
6 May	– Hendon	400m-relay	–	47.4
21 May	Invitation Meeting – Milan	2000m	1st	5:10.6
24 May	Philips Night of Athletics – Crystal Palace	3000m	2nd	7:48.0
1st – H. Rono 7:43.8				
26 May	– Belfast	800m	1st	1:49.0
3 Jun.	– Crystal Palace	2000m	1st	4:57.8*
**UK record*				
10 Jun.	UK v GDR – Crystal Palace	1500m	1st	3:53.8
2nd – J. Straub				
4 Jul.	Invitation Meeting – Cork	Mile	1st	4:08.2
11 Jul.	Invitation Meeting – Dublin	Mile	1st	3:55.7
22 Jul.	– Parliament Hill	400m	1st	48.4
22 Jul.	– Parliament Hill	400m-relay	–	47.3
26 Jul.	Invitation Meeting – Malmo	1500m	1st	3:37.6
27 Jul.	Invitation Meeting – Turku, Finland	800m	1st	1:45.4
3 Aug.	Invitation meeting – Oslo	1500m	1st	3:35.8
19 Aug.	National League Meeting – Brighton	100m	2nd	11.5
19 Aug.	National League Meeting – Brighton	200m	1st	22.9
19 Aug.	National League Meeting – Brighton	1500m	1st	4:08.1

Date	Meeting/Track	Event	Position	Performance
19 Aug.	National League Meeting – Brighton	400m-relay	–	47.4
23 Aug.	Rotary Watches Meeting – Crystal Palace	Mile	1st	3:57.7
29 Aug.	European Champs. – Prague	800m-heat	1st	1:47.8
30 Aug.	European Champs. – Prague	800m-semi	1st	1:46.5
31 Aug.	European Champs. – Prague	800m-final	2nd	1:44.1
**UK record 1st – O. Beyer 1:43.8; 3rd – S. Coe 1:44.8*				
2 Sept.	European Champs. – Prague	1500m-heat	1st	3:42.9
3 Sept.	European Champs. – Prague	1500m-final	1st	3:35.6
15 Sept.	IAC/Coca Cola Meeting – Crystal Palace	2 Miles	1st	8:13.5*
**World outdoor best*				
20 Sept.	Invitation Meeting – Oslo	Mile	1st	3:52.8*
**UK record*				
25 Sept.	Invitation Meeting – Tokyo	Golden Mile	1st	3:55.5

1979 (age twenty-three)

Date	Meeting/Track	Event	Position	Performance
20 May	– Tullyease	2000m	1st	5:20.8
26 May	– Crystal Palace	1500m	1st	3:53.1
26 May	– Crystal Palace	400m-relay	–	48.0
9 Jun.	National League Meeting – Enfield	1500m	1st	3:40.8
9 Jun.	National League Meeting – Enfield	400m-relay	–	47.8
23 Jun.	UK v W. Germ. v Pol. v Switz – Bremen	1500m	1st	3:41.7
24 Jun.	Invitation Meeting – Nijmegen	1500m	1st	3:37.7
10 Jul.	Invitation Meeting – Dublin	800m	1st	1:46.2
13 Jul.	AAA Champs. – Crystal Palace	1500m-heat	1st	3:44.6
14 Jul.	AAA Champs. – Crystal Palace	1500m-final	1st	3:39.1

Date	Meeting/Track	Event	Position	Performance
29 Jul.	National League Meeting – Hendon	1500m	1st	3:46.2
28 Jul.	National League Meeting – Hendon	400m-relay	–	47.3
7 Aug.	Invitation Meeting – Gothenburg	1500m	1st	3:36.6
8 Aug.	– Crystal Palace	1000m	1st	2:23.4
15 Aug.	– Crystal Palace	600m	1st	1:16.0
17 Aug.	Invitation Meeting – West Berlin	Mile	1st	3:54.1
18 Aug.	Invitation Meeting – Crystal Palace	800m-relay	–	1:49.8
19 Aug.	Invitation Meeting – Cologne	800m	2nd	1:45.0
1st – J. Robinson				
27 Aug.	– Crystal Palace	800m	1st	1:49.6
27 Aug.	– Crystal Palace	400m-relay	–	47.0
31 Aug.	Rotary Watches – Crystal Palce	Mile	1st	3:49.6
3:34.0 at 1500m				
4 Sept.	Ivo Van Damme Memorial Meeting – Brussels	1500m	1st	3:32.11
6 Sept.	Invitation Meeting – Koblenz	1000m	1st	2:16.0*
**UK record*				
9 Sept.	Gateshead Games	Emsley Carr Mile	1st	3:56.6
14 Sept.	IAC/Coca Cola Meeting – Crystal Palace	Mile	1st	3:55.3
	1980 (age twenty-four)			
30 Apr.	– Crystal Palace	400m-relay	–	48.2
3 May	Invitation Meeting – Houston, Texas	3000m	1st	7:52.44
9 May	Invitation Meeting – Kingston, Jamaica	1500m	1st	3:38.7
18 May	England v Wales v Hung. v Holl. – Cwmbran	800m	1st	1:49.17
18 May	England v Wales v Hung. v Holl. – Cwmbran	400m-relay	–	47.6
21 May	Philips Night of Athletics – Crystal Palace	Bannister Mile	1st	4:00.6

Date	Meeting/Track	Event	Position	Performance
24 May		600m	1st	76.8
4 Jun.	Invitation Meeting – Bergen	800m	1st	1:46.6
27 Jun.	Talbot Games – Crystal Palace	1500m	1st	3:35.3
1 Jul.	Bislett Games – Oslo	Mile	1st	3:48.8*
*World record				
3 July	Invitation Meeting – Gothenburg	800m	1st	1:48.16
6 Jul.	Open Meeting – Welwyn Garden City	3000m	1st eq.	8:24.6
1st eq. – J. Espir				
15 Jul.	Oslo Games – Oslo	1500m	1st	3:32.09*
*Eq. World record				
24 Jul.	Olympic Games – Moscow	800m-heat	1st	1:49.4
25 Jul.	Olympic Games – Moscow	800m-semi	1st	1:46.6
26 Jul.	Olympic Games – Moscow	800m-final	1st	1:45.4
2nd – S. Coe 1:45.9				
30 Jul.	Olympic Games – Moscow	1500m-heat	1st	3:36.8
31 Jul.	Olympic Games – Moscow	1500m-semi	1st	3:43.1
1 Aug.	Olympic Games – Moscow	1500m-final	3rd	3:49.0
1st – S Coe 3:38.4; 2nd – J. Straub 3.38.8 (Ovett's first 1500m loss since 1977)				
8 Aug.	IAC/Coca Cola Meeting – Crystal Palace	5000m	2nd	13:27.9
1st – J Treacy 13:27.9				
11 Aug.	Invitation Meeting – Budapest	5000m	1st	13:31.94
15 Aug.	Invitation Meeting – Lausanne	1500m	1st	3:35.4
25 Aug.	British Meat Games – Crystal Palace	Golden Mile	1st	3:52.84
27 Aug.	Invitation Meeting – Klobenz	1500m	1st	3:31.36*
*World record				
5 Sept.	AAA Champs. – Crystal Palace	Mile-heat	1st	4:07.9

Date	Meeting/Track	Event	Position	Performance
6 Sept.	AAA Champs. – Crystal Palace	Mile-final	1st	4:04.4
	1981 (age twenty-five)			
24 May	UK Champs. – Antrim	1500m-heat	1st	3:45.1
25 May	UK Champs. – Antrim	1500m-final	1st	3:42.80
3 Jun.	Philips Night of Athletics – Crystal Palace	3000m	1st	7:54.11
7 Jun.	Citizen Games – Gateshead	Mile	1st	3:57.92
17 Jun.	Invitation Meeting – Venice	1000m	1st	2:21.84
26 Jun.	Bislett Games – Oslo	1500m	2nd	3:39.53
1st – T. Byers 3:39.01				
4 Jul.	Europa Cup semi-final – Helsinki	1500m	1st	3:46.47
8 Jul.	Invitation Meeting – Milan	1500m	1st	3:31.95
11 Jul.	Dulux Oslo Games – Oslo	Dream Mile	1st	3:49.25
3:34.1 at 1500m				
14 Jul.	Invitation Meeting – Lausanne	Mile	1st	3:49.66
3:33.34 at 1500m				
26 Jul.	Gateshead Games	800m	1st	1:47.96
29 Jul.	Invitation Meeting – Budapest	1500m	1st	3:31.57
31 Jul.	Talbot Games – Crystal Palace	1000m	1st	2:20.67
3 Aug.	Invitation Meeting – Bergen	1500m	1st	3:34.63
21 Aug.	Invitation Meeting – West Berlin	Mile	1st	3:55.58
26 Aug.	Invitation Meeting – Klobenz	Mile	1st	3:48.40*
**World record*				
29 Aug.	England v Norway – Ardal, Norway	800m	1st	1:47.0
31 Aug.	Amoco Games – Crystal Palace	800m	1st	1:46.40
5 Sept.	World Cup – Rome	1500m	1st	3:34.95

Date	Meeting/Track	Event	Position	Performance
9 Sept.	Invitation Meeting – Reiti	Mile	2nd	3:50.23
1st – S. Maree 3:48.83 (Ovett's first mile loss since 1975)				
11 Sept.	IAC/Coca Cola Meeting – Crystal Palace	2 Mile	1st	8:25.52
3 Oct.	Commonwealth Games Preview – Brisbane	800m	1st	1:49.13
7 Oct.	International Meeting – Adelaide	1500m	1st	3:42.6
10 Oct.	International Meeting – Sydney	Mile	1st	3:59.8
13 Oct.	Burnside Games – Adelaide	1500m	1st	3:42.68

1982 (age twenty-six)

Date	Meeting/Track	Event	Position	Performance
20 Jun.	Southern Champs. – Crystal Palace	1500m-heat	1st	3:47.25
26 Jun.	Bislett Games – Oslo.	3000m	2nd	7:43.87
1st – S.Nyambui 7:43.12				
30 Jun.	Invitation Meeting – Budapest	2000m	1st	5:05.75
7 Jul.	Oslo Games – Oslo	2000	1st	4:57.71*
** UK record*				
9 Jul.	Sport 2000 Meeting – Paris	1500m		Dropped out.
1st – M.Boit				
17 Jul.	Citizen Games – Crystal Palace	3000m	10th	7:48.07
1st – D.Moorcroft 7:32.79 European Record				
31 Jul.	England International – Meadowbank	800m	1st	1:47.59
7 Aug.	BAAB Golden Jubilee Games – Crystal Palace	1500m	1st	3:38.48
11 Aug.	Invitation Meeting – Cologne	800m	2nd	1:46.08
1st – H.Schmid 1:45.90